PRACTICING SKILLS, STRATEGIES & PROCESSES

CLASSROOM TECHNIQUES TO HELP STUDENTS DEVELOP PROFICIENCY

D1495726

PRACTICING SKILLS, STRATEGIES & PROCESSES

CLASSROOM TECHNIQUES TO HELP STUDENTS DEVELOP PROFICIENCY

Kelly Harmon
Robert J. Marzano

With Kathy Marx and Ria A. Schmidt

1400 Centrepark Blvd, Suite 1000
West Palm Beach, FL 33401
717-845-6300

email: pub@learningsciences.com
learningsciences.com

Printed in the United States of America
20 19 18 17 16 15   2 3 4

Publisher's Cataloging-in-Publication Data

Harmon, Kelly.
  Practicing skills, strategies & processes : classroom techniques to help students develop proficiency / Kelly Harmon [and] Robert J. Marzano.
    pages cm. – (Essentials for achieving rigor series)
  ISBN: 978-1-941112-07-6 (pbk.)
1. Learning strategies—Handbooks, manuals, etc. 2. Effective teaching—United States. 3. Thought and thinking—Study and teaching. 4. Critical thinking—Study and teaching. I. Marzano, Robert J. II. Title.
  LB1025.3 .H3766 2014
  370.15—dc23
                              [2015933534]

MARZANO CENTER

Essentials for Achieving Rigor SERIES

The *Essentials for Achieving Rigor* series of instructional guides helps educators become highly skilled at implementing, monitoring, and adapting instruction. Put it to practical use immediately, adopting day-to-day examples as models for application in your own classroom.

Books in the series:

Identifying Critical Content: Classroom Techniques to Help Students Know What is Important

Examining Reasoning: Classroom Techniques to Help Students Produce and Defend Claims

Recording & Representing Knowledge: Classroom Techniques to Help Students Accurately Organize and Summarize Content

Examining Similarities & Differences: Classroom Techniques to Help Students Deepen Their Understanding

Processing New Information: Classroom Techniques to Help Students Engage With Content

Revising Knowledge: Classroom Techniques to Help Students Examine Their Deeper Understanding

Practicing Skills, Strategies & Processes: Classroom Techniques to Help Students Develop Proficiency

Engaging in Cognitively Complex Tasks: Classroom Techniques to Help Students Generate & Test Hypotheses Across Disciplines

Creating & Using Learning Targets & Performance Scales: How Teachers Make Better Instructional Decisions

Organizing for Learning: Classroom Techniques to Help Students Interact Within Small Groups

Dedication

To the people in my life who get me:

Randi Anderson—Thank you for listening to me and giving me so many ideas and resources for this book. You are awesome!

My husband, Jack—You are so patient, kind, and encouraging. Thank you for keeping me going with all your love.

—Kelly Harmon

Table of Contents

Acknowledgments

Learning Sciences International would like to thank the following reviewers:

Gary Abud, Jr.
2014 Michigan Teacher of the Year
Grosse Pointe North High School
Grosse Pointe Woods, Michigan

Randi Anderson
Fourth-Grade Teacher
Elkins Elementary
Ft. Worth, Texas

Jennifer George
Instructional Coach
Floresville South Elementary
Floresville, Texas

Megan Olivia Hall
2014 Minnesota Teacher of the Year
Open World Learning Community
St. Paul, Minnesota

Tara Jacobs
Instructional Coach
Floresville North Elementary
Floresville, Texas

Robin Oliveri
2014 Florida Teacher of the Year
    finalist
Godby High School
Tallahassee, Florida

Angela Romano
Learning Sciences International

Deana Senn
Learning Sciences International

Kimberly Shearer
2012 Kentucky Teacher of the Year
Boone County High School
Florence, Kentucky

Lisa Staats
2012 North Carolina Teacher of the
    Year finalist
Chocowinity Middle Schools
Chocowinity, North Carolina

About the Authors

KELLY HARMON, MAEd, is passionate about reaching learners with diverse needs. For the past 20+ years, Kelly has worked with at-risk learners and their teachers as a classroom teacher, instructional coach, and staff developer. She has presented seminars, institutes, and conferences to more than 10,000 educators during the last 14 years. Kelly helps educators connect with their learners' natural learning modalities, curiosities, and strengths. She assists schools in designing effective curriculum and instruction that matches the standards to best practices. She is married and has six children (three by birth and three by marriage), two grandsons, and three poodles. Kelly loves traveling and learning about interesting places and people.

ROBERT J. MARZANO, PhD, is CEO of Marzano Research Laboratory and Executive Director of the Learning Sciences Marzano Center for Teacher and Leader Evaluation. A leading researcher in education, he is a speaker, trainer, and author of more than 150 articles on topics such as instruction, assessment, writing and implementing standards, cognition, effective leadership, and school intervention. He has authored over 30 books, including *The Art and Science of Teaching* (ASCD, 2007) and *Teacher Evaluation That Makes a Difference* (ASCD, 2013).

KATHLEEN MARX, MSEd, is a leading expert in personal development across industries. She has successfully assisted many districts nationally with implementing deep school improvement changes through her work with Learning Sciences International.

RIA A. SCHMIDT, PhD, has experience as a teacher and administrator, as well as in creating/presenting PD sessions on a variety of topics, guiding district transitions from traditional to standards-based education, and coordinating use of assessments and data for informing instruction.

Introduction

This guide, *Practicing Skills, Strategies & Processes: Classroom Techniques to Help Students Develop Proficiency* is intended as a resource for improving a specific element of instructional practice: *practicing skills, strategies, and processes.*

Your motivation to incorporate this strategy into your instructional toolbox may have come from a personal desire to improve your instructional practice through the implementation of a research-based set of strategies (such as those found in the Marzano instructional framework) or a desire to increase the rigor of the instructional strategies you implement in your class so that students meet the expectations of demanding standards such as the Common Core State Standards, Next Generation Science Standards, C3 Framework for Social Studies State Standards, or state standards based on or influenced by College and Career Readiness Anchor Standards.

This guide will help teachers of all grade levels and subjects improve their performance of a specific instructional strategy: practicing skills, strategies, and processes. Narrowing your focus on a specific skill, such as practicing skills, strategies, and processes, allows you to concentrate on the nuances of this instructional strategy to deliberately improve it. This allows you to intentionally plan, implement, monitor, adapt, and reflect on this single element of your instructional practice. A person seeking to become an expert displays distinctive behaviors, as explained by Marzano and Toth (2013):

- breaks down the specific skills required to be an expert

- focuses on improving those particular critical skill chunks (as opposed to easy tasks) during practice or day-to-day activities

- receives immediate, specific, and actionable feedback, particularly from a more experienced coach

- continually practices each critical skill at more challenging levels with the intention of mastering it, giving far less time to skills already mastered

This series of guides will support each of the previously listed behaviors, with a focus on breaking down the specific skills required to be an expert and giving day-to-day practical suggestions to enhance these skills.

Building on the Marzano Instructional Model

This series is based on the Marzano instructional framework, which is grounded in research and provides educators with the tools they need to connect instructional practice to student achievement. The series uses key terms that are specific to the Marzano model of instruction. See Table 1, Glossary of Key Terms.

Table 1: Glossary of Key Terms

Term	Definition
CCSS	Common Core State Standards is the official name of the standards documents developed by the Common Core State Standards Initiative (CCSSI), the goal of which is to prepare students in the United States for college and career.
CCR	College and Career Readiness Anchor Standards are broad statements that incorporate individual standards for various grade levels and specific content areas.
Desired result	The intended result for the student(s) due to the implementation of a specific strategy.
Monitoring	The act of checking for evidence of the desired result of a specific strategy while the strategy is being implemented.
Instructional strategy	A category of techniques used for classroom instruction that has been proven to have a high probability of enhancing student achievement.
Instructional technique	The method used to teach and deepen understanding of knowledge and skills.
Content	The knowledge and skills necessary for students to demonstrate standards.
Scaffolding	A purposeful progression of support that targets cognitive complexity and student autonomy to reach rigor.
Extending	Activities that move students who have already demonstrated the desired result to a higher level of understanding.

The educational pendulum swings widely from decade to decade. Educators move back and forth between prescriptive checklists and step-by-step lesson plans to approaches that encourage instructional autonomy with minimal regard for the science of teaching and need for accountability. Two practices are often missing in both of these approaches to defining effective instruction: 1) specific statements of desired results, and 2) solid research-based connections. The Marzano instructional framework provides a comprehensive system that details what is required from teachers to develop their craft using research-based instructional strategies. Launching from this solid instructional foundation, teachers will then be prepared to merge that science with their own unique, yet effective, instructional style, which is the art of teaching.

Practicing Skills, Strategies & Processes: Classroom Techniques to Help Students Develop Proficiency will help you grow into an innovative and highly skilled teacher who is able to implement, scaffold, and extend instruction to meet a range of student needs.

Essentials for Achieving Rigor

This series of guides details essential classroom strategies to support the complex shifts in teaching that are necessary for an environment where academic rigor is a requirement for all students. The instructional strategies presented in this series are essential to effectively teach the CCSS, Next Generation Science Standards, or standards designated by your school district or state. They require a deeper understanding, more effective use of strategies, and greater frequency of implementation for your students to demonstrate the knowledge and skills required by rigorous standards. This series includes instructional techniques appropriate for all grade levels and content areas. The examples contained within are grade-level specific and should serve as models and launching points for application in your own classroom.

Your skillful implementation of these strategies is essential to your students' mastery of the CCSS or other rigorous standards, no matter the grade level or subject you are teaching. Other instructional strategies covered in the Essentials for Achieving Rigor series, such as analyzing errors in reasoning and engaging students in cognitively complex tasks, exemplify the cognitive complexity needed to meet rigorous standards. Taken as a package, these strategies may at first glance seem quite daunting. For this reason, the series focuses on just one strategy in each guide.

Practicing Skills, Strategies, and Processes

Practice is the gradual shaping of a skill, strategy, or process over the course of multiple repetitions to some level of proficiency. You have likely experienced several aspects of practice if you have become proficient in a recreational or competitive sport such as golf, swimming, or tennis. First, you had to acquire a variety of facts and concepts—history of the sport, rules of the game, and recommended equipment, as well as the best books and periodicals to read. All of this background knowledge developed a cognitive foundation from which to launch your mastery of the psychomotor processes of the sport. You may have been privileged to work with coaches as they modeled certain strokes and then carefully monitored your moves, providing immediate correction of any errors you made while they moved or positioned your body to set you up for the correct stance or stroke. You were thrilled when you reached the point of independent practice and hopeful that you might achieve fluency in executing all of the discrete skills as a complete package. Practice to proficiency for your students is similar. Practice of critical content is an ongoing, gradual release process that begins with students acquiring and processing the facts, concepts, or principles underlying some type of procedural knowledge, observing a proficient model, and then practicing to proficiency.

Effective teachers have always recognized the need for adequate practice of certain key skills, strategies, and processes. However, they are often conflicted about when and how to organize instruction to provide the needed opportunities for practice. The techniques in this book offer some ways to more effectively structure opportunities for practice in your classroom.

The Effective Implementation of Providing Practice to Proficiency

There is a popular lesson sequence that teachers widely use. Generally known as "I do it, we do it, you do it," this three-step plan captures the essence of effective practice, but none of its nuances. The effective implementation of providing practice to proficiency requires an understanding of the relationship between declarative and procedural knowledge, as well as an understanding of the sequence or flow of the various aspects of practice.

The Relationship Between Procedural Knowledge and Declarative Knowledge

While this book is specifically written to help you effectively implement the practice of procedural knowledge, keep in mind the close relationship that exists between procedural and declarative knowledge. Declarative knowledge consists of the facts, concepts, and generalizations students need to know about content. Procedural knowledge consists of the skills, strategies, and processes students need to be able to do or demonstrate. Procedural knowledge is always rooted in some aspect of declarative knowledge. Although the title and techniques of this book refer specifically to the skills, strategies, and processes that constitute procedural knowledge, never overlook that the acquisition of procedural knowledge always begins with the teaching of its inherent declarative knowledge.

The Critical Aspects of Practice

The effective implementation of providing students with opportunities to practice procedural knowledge to proficiency requires an understanding of the sequence or flow of the various steps necessary for effective practice. The term *sequence* suggests that practice must follow a certain set of steps akin to walking up a set of stairs to reach the top. The term *flow*, on the other hand, suggests that the process of practice can move freely from one place to another making unhindered and steady progress, somewhat like a river—sometimes rushing, sometimes meandering. In reality, practicing procedural knowledge is a little bit of both. However, to effectively help your students practice procedural knowledge to proficiency, you must understand all aspects of the process and implement all of them faithfully as the needs of your students dictate.

The sequence necessary for effective practice includes the following:

1. The teacher models the procedural knowledge.

2. The teacher guides students as they work to replicate the teacher's model.

3. The teacher monitors students and corrects any errors they make, providing additional opportunities to repeat the execution of the skill in more frequent structured practice sessions.

4. As students become more proficient, the teacher provides varied opportunities for students to combine discrete skills or strategy steps together into more complex processes such as writing an essay or editing one's own work.

5. Students engage in independent practice to build fluency for skills that need automaticity, such as skilled reading, or to enhance their controlled processing, that requires students to combine various skills at a more conscious level.

6. Students reflect on their practice.

7. Students repeat the practice as often as needed.

Modeling

Modeling is the most critical, yet overlooked, aspect of practicing critical content. If you are overly eager to dive into the talking and telling parts of practice and skip the showing and doing, practice will be far less productive. Teaching students how to do things requires that you show them how an expert does it. Your role in implementing practice is to model how to execute a skill or process. In cases of more complex procedural knowledge, your modeling should take the form of thinking aloud for students. If you skip the modeling in the interest of time, you will limit your students' opportunities to learn.

Guiding

In this aspect of practice, you become the guide, hence the term *guided practice.* Once you have modeled, you cannot just give students a practice assignment and move on to another group. You must continue to demonstrate and prompt students as they work to replicate your model. The time you spend guiding is a wise investment that will pay rich dividends in terms of students' mastery of critical skills, strategies, and processes.

Monitoring and Correcting

While you are modeling and guiding, you are simultaneously closely monitoring and correcting. The adage that *practice makes perfect* is somewhat erroneous. Only *perfect practice makes perfect.* Each repetition that occurs in the course of the various kinds of practice must be as accurate as possible. Imperfect practice without systematic error correction or specific feedback and modeling will lead to students' gradually shaping and developing incorrect and inefficient skills, strategies, and processes. Once imperfect practice becomes permanent, you and your students must then double down to relearn the skill or process, often delaying their progress toward proficiency.

Combining Discrete Skills Into More Complex Processes

As students become more skilled, teachers provide varied opportunities for them to practice combining discrete skills or individual strategy steps together into more complex processes. At this point in the practice sequence, expect your students to understand the big picture so they can understand that mastering one discrete skill is not your learning target. The combination of these skills and strategies into more complex processes is the goal. Gradually release them to begin shaping and fine-tuning a complex process to make it their own.

Automatic or Controlled Processing

Practice to develop fluency is the final aspect of mastering procedural knowledge. Procedural knowledge developed to automaticity means that students are able to execute a process without giving it any conscious thought. This degree of automaticity enables students' working memories to deal with more complex processes. Controlled processing, on the other hand, takes more conscious attention to a process and involves more thought and decision making about what to do next and how to do it. Processes that initially require more controlled processing can eventually become more automatic after extensive practice, but achieving that level of fluency may be well beyond the scope of your classroom.

Reflection

Ideally, you will be asking your students to reflect on their learning regularly in the process of practice. When you engage your students in the reflection process, they will become more engaged in practicing to proficiency.

Repetition

At the heart of practice is repetition. The more students engage in productive independent practice, the more they begin to shape their own execution of various kinds of procedural knowledge. Some students may fall in love with a certain type of procedural knowledge and be willing to practice beyond perfection. However, for *all* students, your role in the sequence and flow of practice is to provide enough opportunities for productive practice so that *all* students are able to master the skills, strategies, and processes they need to succeed at the next grade level and beyond their formal education.

The following teacher behaviors are associated with planning and implementing effective practice techniques for procedural knowledge in the classroom:

- identifying critical content that is foundational to the procedural knowledge

- facilitating the processing of this critical content

- directly instructing and modeling new skills, strategies, and processes

- providing close monitoring and structured practice at the outset of teaching a new skill, strategy, or process

- correcting errors students make and presenting correct examples immediately

- matching practice activities to students' current skill levels

- gradually decreasing the amount of support provided to students

- gradually increasing the complexity of practice tasks as students become more fluent with new critical content

There are several common mistakes the teacher can make while seeking to become skilled at implementing this instructional strategy:

- The teacher fails to teach inherent conceptual knowledge before scheduling practice of procedural skills.

- The teacher fails to assess students' skill levels before scheduling practice.

- The teacher fails to release responsibility to students for independent practice.

Failing to Teach Conceptual Knowledge in Advance of Scheduling Practice

As noted previously, all types of procedural knowledge, whether discrete skills, strategies, or more complex processes, are based on declarative knowledge. In efforts to cover material and hurry students through the acquisition of procedural knowledge, teachers often feel pressured to shortchange the teaching of declarative knowledge that will enable students to fully understand the nuances of a specific skill, strategy, or process. As a result, practice, rather than deepening students' ability to demonstrate procedural knowledge, fosters rote learning.

Failing to Assess Students' Skill and Knowledge Levels in Advance of Scheduling Practice

The assessment of students' conceptual understanding and current skill levels is essential to planning productive practice. Students who are assigned a practice task for which they have no background knowledge or prior practice will struggle in frustration, while students who have a solid conceptual understanding of the skill, strategy, or process and can execute a procedure will not lose valuable instructional opportunities.

Failing to Release Responsibility to Students for Independent Practice

The ultimate goal of all practice activities is to move students toward mastery of procedural knowledge. They will achieve that goal only if teachers structure increasingly more challenging practice activities and then expect students to take responsibility for their own learning.

Monitoring for the Desired Result

The effective implementation of practicing skills, strategies, and processes requires more than merely providing students with opportunities for practice. Effective implementation also includes monitoring. Monitoring is checking for evidence of the desired result of the strategy during implementation. In other words, effective implementation of a strategy includes monitoring for the desired result of that strategy in real time. The essential question is did your students develop confidence and competence during their practice sessions? A more specific question to be addressed is, was the desired result of the strategy achieved? The most elaborately planned lessons can be exercises in futility unless they begin with instructional strategies in mind, focus on the standards, and are monitored by the teacher for the desired results.

There are multiple ways teachers can monitor whether the majority of students are achieving the desired results of practicing skills, strategies, and processes. Here are some ways to tell if your students are increasing their accuracy and automaticity executing skills, strategies, and processes: .

- Students can perform skills, strategies, and processes with increased confidence.

- Students perform skills, strategies, and processes with increased competence.

- Formative data indicates that students are able to tackle increasingly rigorous tasks with accuracy and automaticity.

- Students can break more complex processes into the appropriate discrete tasks.

- Students need little, if any, support to successfully complete tasks involving the target skills, strategies, and processes.

Scaffolding and Extending Instruction to Meet Students' Needs

As you monitor for the desired result of each purposefully planned practice session, consider how you can meet the needs of some students for additional support as well as the needs of students who have already mastered the expectations for the grade level or course. Planning ahead prevents wasted time and facilitates engaged learning. Within each technique in the subsequent chapters, there are examples of how to intentionally adjust the technique to meet the needs of all learners. You will find examples of ways to provide additional teacher or peer support, how to break down practice into digestible chunks, and how to use materials to adjust for the learners' entry point into the skill, strategy, or process.

Teacher Self-Reflection

As you develop expertise in designing and implementing practice opportunities for your students, reflecting on what works and does not work can help you become more successful in the implementation of this strategy. Use the following set of reflection questions to guide you.

1. How can you regularly provide students with meaningful practice opportunities?

2. How can you demonstrate to students the importance of practice in their acquisition of critical content?

3. How can you monitor your students' mastery of skills, strategies, or processes?

4. What are some ways to create new techniques for providing practice opportunities to address unique student needs and situations?

5. What are you learning about your students as you adapt and create new techniques?

Instructional Techniques to Help Students Practice Skills, Strategies, and Processes

There are many ways to help your students master critical skills, strategies, and processes through practice. These ways or options are called *instructional techniques*. They are described in two categories: guided practice and independent practice.

Part I: Guided Practice

Instructional Technique 1: Close Monitoring

Instructional Technique 2: Worked Examples

Instructional Technique 3: Frequent Structured Practice

Part II: Independent Practice

Instructional Technique 4: Fluency Practice

Instructional Technique 5: Varied Practice

Instructional Technique 6: Practice Before Tests

All of the techniques are similarly organized and include the following components:

- a brief introduction to the technique

- ways to effectively implement the technique

- common mistakes to avoid as you implement the technique

- examples and nonexamples from elementary and secondary classrooms using selected learning targets or standards

- ways to monitor for the desired result

- ways to scaffold and extend instruction to meet the needs of students

PART I

GUIDED PRACTICE

As previously stated, the practice of critical content is an ongoing, gradual release process. Think of the practice of skills, strategies, and processes as a continuum along which you begin with a strong presence and close attention to the progress of your students. Your active presence and close attention characterize the category of guided practice. The role you play in guiding the practice activity defines the techniques in this category.

Instructional Technique 1

CLOSE MONITORING

The technique of close monitoring is characterized by a highly structured period of practice in which you observe your students practicing. Close monitoring is essential during the beginning stages of acquiring critical content. Students need guided practice with a teacher or coach who is closely watching their responses to explicit instruction and teacher modeling. During close monitoring, students receive feedback and reinforcement of their correct approximations of the skill and immediate correction of any errors or misunderstandings. Since practice makes permanent, ensure that your students practice accurately from the beginning. Following the initial instruction of any type of procedural knowledge, students will need to execute the initial skill, strategy, or process several times, depending on the ease and speed with which they progress. Close monitoring can occur at any grade level or in any content area, and it is critical when students are beginning to learn the first discrete skills in a process or steps in a strategy and need closer supervision and scaffolding to master those skills.

How to Effectively Implement Close Monitoring

The effective implementation of close monitoring depends on your understanding of and close attention to several variables as you plan and then implement this technique:

- Grouping students in ways that facilitates close monitoring

- Explicitly instructing the key concepts and vocabulary that are foundational to the target skill or process

- Providing opportunities to process the key concepts and vocabulary

- Modeling that shows students how to execute the skill or thinking aloud that shows students how to use a cognitive process

- Successfully practicing immediately following modeling

Table 1.1 contains a template that shows how to effectively implement close monitoring during practice. The template is divided into three parts. Part 1 of the template describes the steps during which you teach the conceptual knowledge that is foundational to the skill. Part 2 describes the steps that lead up to the practice session. These steps include the instructional decisions you make before you are fully prepared to put the practice session in your plan book. Part 3 describes the actual practice session. Column 1 describes each of the steps, while Column 2 provides explanatory notes for the teacher.

Table 1.1: Sample Lesson Template for Effectively Implementing Close Monitoring

PART 1: Teach the Conceptual Knowledge That Is Inherent in the Skill, Strategy, or Process	
Implementation	Explanatory Notes for the Teacher
1. Select the learning target for which you will implement close monitoring during practice.	Practice should always be connected to the learning target you select. Hastily chosen practice from a workbook or website can easily become nothing more than a way to keep students busy that does not produce the desired result.
2. Identify the critical content that you will initially teach your students prior to the practice session.	Identify the vocabulary and concepts that students need to understand before they can practice meaningfully.
3. Identify the ways in which students will process the critical content they need to understand as a foundation for practicing the skill.	Once you have introduced the conceptual knowledge, engage students in processing it in a variety of ways.
PART 2: Do Before Your Practice Session	
1. Determine how you will monitor students' performance of the skill, strategy, or process.	Close monitoring is immediate monitoring that enables you to correct an error, ask a guiding question, or point students in a more productive direction. Small groups are the most productive way to closely monitor.
2. Determine how you will chunk the skill, strategy, or process to make it more manageable.	Begin with the smallest chunk or step of a skill, strategy, or process to give your students a greater likelihood of experiencing immediate success during their first practice session.

3. If appropriate for the skill, strategy, or process as well as for the grade and content, prepare an anchor chart that gives students visual cues for reviewing the steps of a skill, strategy, or process.	Anchor charts should include a definition or description and the steps for executing a skill, strategy, or process. In addition to anchor charts, consider preparing a handout for students to consult. This handout can be useful during later independent practice sessions.
4. Develop a menu of guiding questions that are appropriate for your grade level and content.	For example, while students practice a math skill, ask the following questions: 1) How should you begin? 2) What do you need to do next? 3) How will you check your work?
PART 3: Practice the Skill, Strategy, or Process	
1. Determine the specific task you want students to practice during the practice session.	Although this sounds simple, this step often takes the most thought. Will the task produce the desired outcome of your learning target? Do students have the essential conceptual knowledge to understand what they are practicing and why? Is the task too complicated? Is the task relevant?
2. Model the task for students.	Show students how to execute a skill, strategy, or process before asking them to do it on their own. Even though you are closely monitoring, your students' first attempts can often establish a pattern of success or frustration.
3. Throughout the practice session, focus on shaping students' conceptual understanding by asking them to explain what they are thinking or why they did what they did.	Rather than telling your students what to do, pose a question, provide another model or demonstration, or think aloud. This approach demands that your students do the thinking and learning.
4. After several opportunities for students to respond in which you have closely monitored their progress, ask students to reflect on their practice session.	As appropriate for your grade level, help your students break down what may not be working for them and what needs to change so they can develop proficiency with a skill, strategy, or process.

Common Mistakes

The implementation of a new technique can often result in unanticipated mistakes. However, knowing ahead of time where problems might arise will increase your likelihood of success in implementing this technique.

Watch out for these common mistakes as you implement close monitoring:

- The teacher fails to set the stage for practice by identifying critical content and giving students opportunities to process it before moving into practice.

- The teacher gives students tasks to practice that are far beyond their current skill levels.

- The teacher gives students too many chunks of new material to handle during initial practice sessions.

- The teacher tells the students what to do or think, rather than prompting the students to attend to the demonstration or think-aloud she provides.

- The teacher does not provide students with adequate think (wait) time.

- The teacher provides a question prompt, but then answers the question.

- The teacher provides too much wait time.

- The teacher expects students to practice isolated skills that are not linked to the context of the overall process.

- The teacher fails to guide the students to self-monitor their progress as their competence and confidence develop.

Examples and Nonexamples of Close Monitoring

The following examples and nonexamples of close monitoring of students' practice may illustrate a different grade level or subject than you teach. View them as you would a fresh perspective from a colleague and consider how you might adapt them in your classroom.

Elementary Example of Close Monitoring

The learning target for this elementary classroom example is: *compose and decompose numbers from 11 to 19 into ten ones and some further ones, e.g., by using objects, and record each composition or decomposition by a drawing or equation* (CCSS.Math.Content K.NBT.A.1). The example demonstrates how to closely monitor students during a kindergarten math lesson guided practice session. The example is divided into two sections: 1) a sample template that will enable you to gain a comprehensive view of the important aspects of a lesson that must occur before a practice session and 2) a classroom scenario describing the specific aspect of the lesson devoted to the close monitoring of practice.

Sample Lesson Template for Implementing Close Monitoring: Kindergarten Math

Table 1.2 is a lesson template showing the steps for the close monitoring of math practice in a kindergarten classroom. The first three steps in Part 1 are about teaching and processing the conceptual knowledge needed prior to practicing the decomposing of numbers. Part 2 describes the actual practice session.

Table 1.2: Sample Lesson Template for Implementing Close Monitoring: Kindergarten Math

PART 1: Teach the Conceptual Knowledge That Is Inherent in the Skill, Strategy, or Process	
Implementation	Explanatory Notes for the Teacher
1. Select the learning target for which you will implement close monitoring during practice.	The learning target for this example is *compose and decompose numbers from 11 to 19 into ten ones and some further ones, e.g., by using objects, and record each composition or decomposition by a drawing or equation* (CCSS.Math.Content K.NBT.A.1).
2. Identify the critical content that you will initially teach your students prior to the practice session.	Students will need to be able to count from 11 to 19 and understand the concept of place value (ones and tens). Students must understand the meanings of the terms *compose* and *decompose* (or take apart). Students need to understand how to record the concept by drawing, writing an equation, or using manipulatives.
3. Identify the ways in which students will process the critical content they need to understand as a foundation for practicing the skill.	Students will process this critical content by counting manipulatives and objects on a page. In a second session, students will process by writing equations that match a pre-prepared drawing of objects. Students will understand the term *digit,* as well as understand what a rod represents and what a unit represents.

(continued on next page)

Table 1.2: Sample Lesson Template for Implementing Close Monitoring: Kindergarten Math *(continued)*

PART 2: Practice the Skill, Strategy, or Process	
Implementation	Explanatory Notes for the Teacher
1. Determine the specific task you want students to practice during the practice session.	Students will, on individual desk mats, decompose numbers from 11 to 19 by placing one base ten rod to represent the number in the tens column and the correct number of units to represent the number in the ones column.
2. Model the task.	Teacher models the process for students, thinking aloud about how she decides which manipulatives to place on her mat to represent the number 19. She thinks aloud to show students how she is checking her work and replaces her materials in the box. She then models the process with another number between 11 and 19.
3. Provide materials to the students and ask them to decompose the number modeled for them.	Students begin practicing and teacher observes, making sure all students in the group are decomposing the number correctly.
4. Coach, prompt, and praise students as appropriate.	Teacher asks students to place their manipulatives in the box and get ready to decompose another number.
5. Have students practice the task three times.	Teacher encourages students to ask questions.
6. When students make errors, correct the errors and ask them to start over and practice the correct layout on their mats.	Students practice each layout three times successfully before the teacher presents a new number for them to decompose.
7. Debrief the students by asking questions regarding their understanding of the skill.	Students report excitement about their success and would like to use the rod and units to decompose the numbers from 10 to 29 the next day.

Classroom Scenario for Implementing Close Monitoring: Kindergarten Math

The kindergarten teacher in this example has been working with her students for several weeks on developing the background knowledge and conceptual understanding they need to practice the skill of using manipulatives. They have been practicing counting from 11 to 19, writing their numbers from 11 to 19, and playing various games. They have previously used rods to help them visualize numbers. The scenario begins as the teacher models the task she wants them to practice today (Table 1.3, Part 2, No. 2).

Boys and girls, we have learned that numbers can be taken apart [decomposed] using the base ten rods and units. We've been working with the numbers 11–19, and I have a set of cards for you that have these numbers written on them. I'm going to use my set of cards to help me pick a number to take apart. *The teacher pulls the number 19 from her set of cards and puts it above her mat.* Watch me as I show you how I decompose the number 19. When I get ready to decompose this number, I first say the number, 19, and then I look in the ones place of that number. I see the number 9, and that tells me this number has nine ones. So, I am going to count out nine units. Watch me. I'm going to put them on my mat.

She counts out the nine units again as she puts them on her math mat.

Now I'm going to look at the number in the tens place. That number is 1 and it stands for ten ones, so I am going to choose one rod that stands for ten ones. Now I am going to check my work. I look at the number in the ones place, a 9, and I count my units to make sure I have nine. *The teacher counts her units aloud.* Now I check the number in the tens place, a 1, and that means I should have one rod, and I do. I have taken apart my number, 19, one ten and nine ones.

After modeling for her students, the teacher introduces the practice session.

Today, you are going to practice taking apart numbers. You each have a mat and some rods and units. First, I want you to take apart the number 19. That's the one I showed you. *The teacher has removed her model to see whether her students are ready to work somewhat independently, although she will closely monitor each student.* Try it. *Her students hesitate, so she prompts them.* Remember you are going to start in the ones place. *The prompt is all they need to start them off. All five students are able to decompose 19. Some do it more quickly than others, and she decides to have them practice 19 one more time.*

Put your rod and units back in the pile above your mat. Show me how you would take apart 19 using your manipulatives. *This time the students complete the task more quickly and all have accurately decomposed 19. The teacher then decides to give them another number between 11 and 19 to practice. She gives them the number 15 and watches as they count and place their rods and units in the correct place on the math mat. She notices that Jeremy's mat looks like the mat in Figure 1.1. She immediately begins to question and prompt Jeremy.* Jeremy, read the number that you are decomposing for me. *Jeremy correctly answers 15.* Good. Now tell me what that 5 means? *Jeremy answers, "Five ones."* Good. Now, go to the ones half of your mat and count the number of ones you have placed there. *Jeremy begins counting and immediately recognizes that he has made an error. The teacher wants to know what Jeremy was thinking when he thought he was finished after placing four units on the mat. Jeremy explains that he was in a hurry and did not check his work by looking at the number in the ones place and then counting the number of units he placed in the ones half of his mat. The teacher asks him to correct his mat.*

Figure 1.1: Jeremy's Mat Showing the Number 14

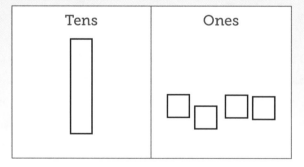

> *The teacher then asks the students to pull a number from their pile of cards and take it apart on their mats using the manipulatives.* Put the number you chose at the top of your mat so I can check your work. *The teacher knows this is a crucial part of the practice session and is closely monitoring her students to make sure that every representation is accurate.*

Elementary Nonexample of Close Monitoring

The nonexample kindergarten teacher in the next room is teaching the same standard. Throughout the small group lesson, he tells students what to think rather than prompting them with questions. The teacher gives them base ten rods and units to use, but does not model decomposing for the group. When the teacher provides the target number 12, he tells the students *"There is a 2 in the ones places, so get two units. There is a 1 in the tens place, so get one rod. Now we have one ten and two ones, or 10 + 2 = 12."* The teacher writes the number 12 on the whiteboard. He gives the students four more target numbers and repeats the sequence. He releases the students to math stations without any reflections or having revised any knowledge. Instead of the teacher guiding practice, the students are merely following directives from the teacher. The nonexample teacher misses a valuable opportunity to develop and shape the students' base ten conceptual knowledge by asking guiding questions.

Secondary Example of Close Monitoring

The secondary example of close monitoring is based on the following learning target: *cite strong and thorough textual evidence to support analysis of what text says explicitly as well as inferences drawn from the text, including determining where the text leaves matters uncertain* (CCSS.ELA-Literacy/ RL/11-12/1). The example demonstrates how a high school teacher closely monitors her students during a guided practice session in an English class. The example is divided into two sections: 1) a sample template that will enable you to follow the lesson steps and 2) a classroom scenario describing the specific aspect of the lesson devoted to the close monitoring of practice.

Sample Lesson Template for Implementing Close Monitoring: Eleventh-Grade ELA

Table 1.3 is a sample lesson template illustrating the secondary example of the close monitoring of practice. Part 1 describes the conceptual knowledge students need to acquire before they can engage in productive practice. The practice session in the scenario is in Part 2.

Table 1.3: Sample Lesson Template for Implementing Close Monitoring: Eleventh-Grade ELA

PART 1: Teach the Conceptual Knowledge That Is Inherent the Skill, Strategy, or Process	
Implementation	Explanatory Notes for the Teacher
1. Select the learning target for which you will implement close monitoring during practice.	The learning target for this example is cite strong and thorough textual evidence to support analysis of what the text says explicitly as well as inferences drawn from the text, including determining where the text leaves matters uncertain.
2. Identify the critical content that you will initially teach your students prior to the practice session.	There is a great deal of critical content inherent in this literacy process: a) an understanding of how to find textual evidence and embed it in the analysis, b) an understanding of what it means to analyze text, and c) an understanding of the terms analysis, develop, textual evidence, and embed.
3. Identify the ways in which students will process the critical content they need to understand as a foundation for practicing the skill.	Students will process this critical content over several weeks by looking at worked examples and nonexamples of embedded textual evidence and learning how to analyze a text.
PART 2: Practice the Skill, Strategy, or Process	
1. Determine the task you want students to practice during their practice session.	Students will find examples of the various ways that authors develop characters, events, or ideas in a short piece of text and then practice writing sentences that embed textual evidence.
2. Prepare any necessary materials to scaffold students in their practice of this process.	Figure 1.2 is an anchor chart to help students move through the steps in the process of embedding textual evidence in their written analysis of a text.

3. Model the task.	Teacher models the process for students by thinking aloud for them about how she would write a sentence that embeds textual evidence into a piece of writing. See Figure 1.3 for a more comprehensive version of the modeling.
4. Students practice and you observe, making sure all students are on track in terms of writing one sentence without evidence and a second sentence with cited evidence.	Teacher walks around the room, stopping and reading what students have written. She coaches, prompts, and praises students as appropriate. If one partner is having more success, she encourages that individual to offer suggestions.
5. Students practice writing another sentence that embeds evidence from the text.	After students have written their first sentence embedding evidence and received an OK from the teacher, they move to the next chunk of text to write another sentence that embeds evidence.

Figure 1.2 is a combination anchor chart/think sheet the teacher has prepared to help her students master the process of finding textual evidence to support a claim they make in their analysis of the text. Once she has modeled the process for them, they can readily follow the steps and then write their responses below each step.

Figure 1.3 is a sample teacher think-aloud showing students how to embed textual evidence. When teachers model a process such as this, students are able to practice with more confidence.

Figure 1.2: Anchor Chart/Think Sheet for Embedding Textual Evidence

1.	Pick out some words and phrases in the test that might illustrate or provide evidence of the point you are trying to make in your statement. You might be trying to support a conclusion you have drawn from the text or evaluate an argument and specific claims the author has made in the text. First, write these words and phrases in the space below (1a). As you write them, think about how you could write your own words and phrases that mean about the same thing.
1a.	
2.	Now, think about and jot down some possible ways you might write an original sentence about the central idea of the text, a conclusion you have drawn about what the text means, or how you want to evaluate an argument or claim the author has made. These ideas are the beginning of the rough draft of your sentence. Write that rough draft in the space below (2a).
2a.	
3.	Now, experiment with placing the words and phrases you selected from the text in step 1 into the ideas you want to have in the sentence you wrote down in step 2. Choose the order so that the words flow smoothly. Sometimes the only way to determine whether the sentence "feels" right is to read it aloud to see how it sounds. Write that sentence in the space below (3a).
3a.	

Adapted from McEwan-Adkins & Burnett (2012).

Figure 1.3: A Sample Teacher Think-Aloud About How to Embed Textual Evidence

One of the skills you need to master as you analyze and write about text is how to select and use quotations from the text to cite as evidence. This kind of evidence is called *textual evidence.*

Yesterday we read an excerpt from a book in which the author was describing his life growing up as a Native American. I first wrote a statement about the text without providing any evidence to support my statement.

Here's what I wrote: *The author develops the text primarily with details about the lessons he learned during his childhood in Virginia.*

I can't use a statement like that in answer to a question or response to a prompt. I have to provide evidence from the text—actual words and phrases that I take out of the text to support my statement.

Here's what I wrote: *The author develops the text primarily with details about lessons he learned to "work hard, say little, and blend in," during his childhood in Virginia to explain why he has a "sketchy" background about his tribe and only "stock answers" for his grandchildren whenever they ask his opinion about Indians.*

The words and phrases with quotation marks around them in the second example are called *embedded quotations.* These words and phrases are directly copied from the original text. You can copy selected words and phrases from an author's work if you put quotation marks around them. These embedded quotations are called *evidence* because they illustrate or prove a statement you make about the author's writing.

Reprinted from McEwan-Adkins & Burnett (2012), with permission. Solution Tree Press. Figure 9.3, How to Embed Textual Evidence.

Classroom Scenario for Implementing Close Monitoring: Eleventh-Grade ELA

A high school English teacher wants her students to master the process of embedding textual evidence and then practice it while she closely monitors their progress. In the past she has given a brief explanation of the process and followed up with a homework assignment for them to turn in the following day. She now realizes that she needs to show her students how to do this by thinking aloud and modeling and then providing opportunities for them to practice doing this under her watchful eye. She has twenty students in her class, a small class size by any standard, but it is still too large for the kind of close monitoring she wants to do for this particular process. She decides to break up the class into two smaller groups of five pairs of students each and will alternate checking in on each group and its set of partners.

She models the process shown in Figure 1.3, using text the students have previously read. She wants them to practice writing one sentence that embeds textual evidence from the second chunk of text. She encourages students to look at the anchor chart to guide their work. The model she provides cites evidence from the first chunk of text. There are two additional chunks of text, and she assigns each pair of partners the second chunk to work on.

Here is how she explains the assignment to students:

> Class, I've modeled this process for you, and you have a copy of the text we've read that was chunked into three parts. There are two chunks left, and I want each of you to write two practice sentences based on the first chunk. I'm going to be walking around the classroom monitoring your work to make sure you are following my model and using the steps in the anchor chart.
>
> *The teacher is pleased that her students are taking this assignment seriously and have really benefited from the modeling and thinking aloud she has provided. Students are helping their partners polish their sentences.*
>
> *Near the end of the period, the teacher interrupts students and calls time.* Thank you, class, for the outstanding effort and quality products you have produced during this class period. I realize that some of you may still be working, but I am going to collect all the papers to look more closely at your work. If you haven't finished, I will give you the option to finish it during your lunch period or study hall and drop it off before you leave for the day.

Secondary Nonexample of Close Monitoring

The nonexample secondary teacher is focused on the same learning target as the example teacher. She uses the same model, sample text, and anchor chart. However, the nonexample teacher fails to teach and then have his students process the conceptual knowledge underlying the skill. Further, he does not believe that all the models and charts are necessary for practicing a simple task like citing evidence to support statements students have made when writing an analysis of a text. He vastly overestimates his students' abilities to master this process. When he sits down to read their papers, he realizes they lack the conceptual background needed to execute the skill, and the quality of their papers was not at all up to the standards of the English department.

Determining If Students Are Proficient in Using Close Monitoring

There are two aspects of monitoring any practice technique: 1) something that students do to demonstrate the desired result of their practice activity and 2) something the teacher does to check for this desired result and respond to students' progress. Here are some specific examples of checking for the desired result during a period of close monitoring:

- Listen carefully as students explain their rationale for the choices they made during practice.

- Listen carefully as students read aloud written products to determine whether they meet the task's criteria for accuracy.

- After demonstrating the skill, strategy, or process, ask students to respond chorally and visually scan the group to determine whether students have responded correctly.

- After it appears that most students are correctly responding chorally, shift to calling on individual students to respond.

- Have students write their responses on whiteboards to demonstrate mastery.

The student proficiency scale for the effectiveness of practice activities during close monitoring is shown in Table 1.4. It will help you assess how well your students are benefiting from the types of practice activities you are using. Use the scale to help you monitor for the desired result of your close monitoring of students' practice.

Table 1.4: Student Proficiency Scale for Practicing Skills, Strategies, and Processes Using Close Monitoring

Emerging	Fundamental	Desired Result
Students watch the teacher model the skill, strategy, or process.	Students attempt the skill, strategy, or process.	Students execute the skill, strategy, or process.
Students can describe the major points of the skill, strategy, or process.	Students can accurately explain the components of the skill, strategy, or process.	Students can explain what they are thinking or why they did what they did.
Students reflect on their practice session.	Students can describe the needed action for success with the skill, strategy, or process.	Students are able to explain what may not be working for them and what needs to change so they can develop proficiency with a skill, strategy, or process.

Scaffold and Extend Instruction to Meet Students' Needs

There will be some students in every class who need more explicit instruction and longer periods of close monitoring. Likewise, there will be students who need little to no monitoring in terms of a particular skill, strategy, or process. Use the following ideas as springboards to create scaffolds and extensions for these students.

Scaffolding

- Provide an anchor chart or flowchart of steps in the skill, strategy, or process. Have the student label the chart with questions that will prompt the accurate behavior. Allow the student to refer to the drawing during the initial practice sessions.

- Have the student create a mnemonic device to remember the steps in the skill.

- Break the skill into smaller chunks and have the students practice then summarize the step. Students should achieve automaticity before moving to the next chunk of the skill.

- Make sure all students are practicing. Have students practice using whiteboards that can be easily displayed and erased.

- When possible, use technology-based student response systems to ensure that all students participate in the practice. If you do not have an interactive whiteboard, use free online student response systems such as Socrative.com or Infuselearning.com. Both systems allow students to use a computer or tablet to record responses that demonstrate understanding of procedural knowledge. You can also save the data from student responses for evidence of understanding and application. Both of the applications allow you to download a report that contains student responses.

Extending

- Provide challenging problems and prompt the students to hypothesize how the use/nonuse of the skill or strategy will impact the outcome.

- Have students make and test predictions about what will happen if the skill, strategy, or process is used in different situations or contexts.

- Have students watch live demonstrations (or videos) or critique exemplars of products in which the skill is being or has been used.

- Have students create a set of criteria for determining the quality of the performance. Students will need to deduce the skill being used and critique the performance for mastery of the procedural knowledge.

Instructional Technique 2

WORKED EXAMPLES

Worked examples are step-by-step demonstrations or models of how to execute a skill, strategy, or process. Worked examples are a type of guided practice and are most effective as a practice technique when students are just beginning to acquire critical content. They come in various formats: a textual model illustrating procedural knowledge in the literacy content of reading and writing, graphically organized steps with illustrations detailing how a specific algorithm works, or colorful animations on the internet that serve to make a scientific process more understandable. There are four primary reasons to consider using worked examples for practice in your classroom: 1) to scaffold the learning of complex procedural knowledge with multiple steps; 2) to reduce students' cognitive load while they are acquiring a new skill, strategy, or process; 3) to guide students' deeper understanding by providing prompts for self-explanation or self-reflection as they work through the examples; and 4) to increase students' background knowledge and strengthen their conceptual knowledge.

While scaffolding is typically thought of as a way to support struggling learners, in the case of using worked examples for practice, think of it as a way to prevent students from becoming discouraged during their initial exposures to challenging procedural knowledge. Roadblocks can pop up in terms of various skills. Consider using worked examples as a way to avoid these roadblocks, thereby giving your students more successful and satisfying first encounters with critical content. Learners who might otherwise give up after the first lesson can replay the video, follow the steps of a text model, or enhance their ability to solve problems with annotated diagrams and examples.

Worked examples are often used in mathematics textbooks, but they can be useful in other content areas as well. The internet provides a multitude of animated worked examples from various content areas. Keep in mind, however, that worked examples may not be appropriate for all learners. Students who have already mastered a skill, strategy, or process can easily become bored if expected to spend too much time in guided practice with a worked example.

How to Effectively Implement Worked Examples

The effective implementation of worked examples involves three basic steps: 1) teaching students the conceptual knowledge that is the basis of the skill, strategy, or process you want them to practice to proficiency; 2) preparing the worked examples, student scripts, or sample self-reflections in advance of the practice session; and 3) modeling how to use the worked example and closely monitoring students' practice.

Teach Conceptual Knowledge Underlying the Skill, Strategy, or Process

The focus of this guide is the practice of skills, strategies, and processes using various techniques. Take the time needed to teach the concepts and vocabulary students must understand to make their practice sessions productive.

Acquire or Develop a Worked Example for the Skill, Strategy, or Process

The most effective worked examples have the following characteristics: 1) are self-explanatory, 2) contain a minimal amount of extraneous material, 3) show relationships between different aspects of the example, 4) highlight structural features that help learners integrate the solution to the problem or execution of a task, and 5) isolate the most meaningful aspects of the example (Renkl, 1997). You can create your own worked examples, use exemplary student work from earlier school years (if the students have granted permission), or locate worked examples on the internet.

There are two features of worked examples that can enhance the practice experience for students: student scripts and self-reflections. Student scripts are written by the teacher and then read aloud by students. The scripts serve as narration to each step of a specific worked example. They are written in the first person using student-friendly language so that as partners take turns reading the script aloud, they can begin to gain fluency in using the language of a skill, strategy, or process and thus conceptualize the steps more deeply. The scripts appear adjacent to each step in the worked example.

Self-reflections are either spoken aloud or written down by students, depending on the needs of the student and your preference as the teacher. Self-reflections are a blend of students "talking to themselves" and "thinking aloud" about what they are doing. They may remind themselves of a rule or be a statement of exactly how they solved a problem or executed a process.

Model and Monitor Using Worked Examples

Model for students how to read a script aloud and carefully go through the steps of the skill, strategy, or process. Also model for students how to reflect on their thinking. Take the time to help students see the purposes the script and self-reflections serve: 1) they ensure students thoroughly rehearse the steps of the strategy or process and 2) they actively engage students in mastery of the procedural knowledge.

Once you have modeled how to use the script as well as how to reflect about their thinking, expect students to work in pairs to practice. Guiding students to this kind of self-reflection requires the type of close monitoring described in Instructional Technique 1. You will want to listen in to determine that students are carefully reading the script as well as to determine if their self-reflections are on target. Figure 2.1, which accompanies the elementary classroom example, contains both a student script the teacher wrote as well as a set of self-reflections the student wrote.

Table 2.1 contains a lesson template for designing practice using worked examples. Part 1 of the template contains the steps during which you will introduce the conceptual knowledge that is the foundation of the skill. Students will then have one or more opportunities to process that content. Part 2 describes the steps that take place to prepare for the practice session, while Part 3 describes the actual practice session.

Table 2.1: Sample Lesson Template for Effectively Implementing Worked Examples

PART 1: Teach the Conceptual Knowledge as the Basis for Acquiring the Skill, Strategy, or Process	
Implementation	Explanatory Notes for the Teacher
1. Select the learning target for your worked example.	The learning target you select should guide the selection of a worked example you will use later in the lesson.
2. Identify the critical content you will initially teach your students prior to introducing the worked example.	Teach the concepts, vocabulary, and background knowledge that will enable students to more readily understand and benefit from using the worked example to practice.
3. Identify the ways in which you will have your students process this critical content.	Your students will need to talk about, write about, and work with the critical content before they will be fully prepared to practice.
PART 2: Do Before Your Practice Session	
1. Locate or develop the worked example that you plan to use.	Begin collecting worked examples so they will be in your file when you are looking for one.
2. If appropriate, write a model script for students to use with the worked example.	Write the model script in the first person so students can read aloud and visually walk through the steps of the process as if they wrote the script. Make it student friendly.
3. Develop some sample self-reflections you can use in your modeling for students.	The students are responsible for writing their own self-reflections, but until you model what that looks and sounds like, they will not likely fully enjoy and benefit from the process.
PART 3: Practice the Skill, Strategy, or Process	
1. Model how you expect students to use the worked example.	Think aloud as you read the student script. Show students what is going on in your mind as you contemplate working out a problem or executing the process shown in the example.
2. Monitor as students use the worked example to more deeply understand the skill, strategy, or process.	Make sure students are individually reading aloud the steps and following them.
3. Provide two problems for students to resolve using the worked example as their model.	Once each student has worked two problems, they pair up to compare answers and self-reflect about the process and whether worked examples were helpful.

Common Mistakes

As with all instructional techniques, there are more and less effective ways to implement practice activities using worked examples. Being aware of the common mistakes in advance of planning your lessons will help you create successful practice experience for your students. Here are some of the common mistakes to avoid:

- The teacher fails to adequately identify critical content related to the worked example and does not provide students with opportunities to process that content prior to the introduction of the worked example.

- The teacher fails to use examples that are accessible to students.

- The teacher fails to expect students to think aloud and reflect as they navigate through the steps of the worked example.

- The teacher fails to provide close monitoring to ensure students are grasping the essence of the skill, strategy, or process.

- The teacher fails to follow up an initial worked example with a second more complex example.

- The teacher provides too many worked examples, thereby confusing students.

- The teacher constructs a worked example that does not adequately exemplify the skill or strategy.

- The teacher focuses on the worked example as the only or best solution.

- The teacher focuses too vigorously on algorithmic skills domains.

- The teacher fails to fade the worked example and replace it with tasks and problems that require students to execute the procedural knowledge more independently.

Examples and Nonexample of Worked Examples

The examples and nonexamples of how teachers have used worked examples in their classrooms may be from a different grade level or subject than you teach. However, you may well find some helpful ideas to spark your own creative approach to using worked examples.

Elementary Example of Worked Examples

This example demonstrates how an elementary teacher uses worked examples as part of guided practice in her fourth-grade math class. The example is divided into two parts: 1) a sample template that will enable you to follow the lesson steps and 2) a classroom scenario describing the specific aspect of the lesson devoted to using worked examples in a practice session.

Sample Lesson Template for Implementing Worked Examples: Fourth-Grade Math

Table 2.2 is a sample lesson template describing the steps for using worked examples to practice in a fourth-grade math classroom.

Table 2.2: Sample Lesson Template for Implementing Worked Examples: Fourth-Grade Math

PART 1: Teach the Conceptual Knowledge That Serves as a Foundation for the Skill, Strategy, or Process	
Implementation	Explanatory Notes for the Teacher
1. Select the learning target for your worked example.	The learning target for this worked example practice lesson is *multiply a whole number of up to four digits by a one-digit whole number, and multiply two two-digit numbers, using strategies based on place value and the properties of operations. Illustrate and explain the calculation by using equations, rectangular arrays, and/or area models* (4.NBT.B.5, CCSS).
2. Identify the critical content you will initially teach your students prior to introducing the worked example.	The critical content includes the concepts of place value and the properties of operations.
3. Give your students opportunities to process the important conceptual knowledge they will need to fully benefit from the worked examples.	Students will process this critical content by illustrating and explaining the calculation using equations, rectangular arrays, and/or area models.
PART 2: Do Before Your Practice Session	
1. Develop the worked example that you plan to use.	The teacher develops a worked example of double-digit multiplication. See Figure 2.1.
2. Develop a model script to demonstrate to students how to talk to themselves or think aloud about the various steps in the task or problem.	The model script is in column 1 of Figure 2.1.

3. Develop a set of self-reflection questions to prompt your students after the practice session.	The teacher also develops a set of sample self-reflections for students to show them how to think about what they are doing as they work. The sample self-reflections are in column 3 of Figure 2.1.
PART 3: Practice the Skill, Strategy, or Process	
1. Model for students how they will use the script to work their way through the example.	The teacher uses the script as part of her think-aloud showing students how to read the script, pointing to the steps in the problem.
2. Once students have read through and processed the worked example, give them two problems to solve following the model of the worked example.	Students can read the provided script as they work through the two practice problems.
3. Use the sample self-reflections to guide your students in reflecting how this practice helps them better understand the process.	The teacher prompts students to talk about how having a script and worked examples helps them better understand the skill.

Figure 2.1: Worked Example of Double-Digit Multiplication With Sample Student Script and Self-Reflections

Student Script for the Worked Example	Worked Example	Self-Reflections
1. The first step is to write down the problem. It does not matter which number goes on top. I also need to put a multiplication sign (×) to the left of the bottom number.	32 × 23	I know that I can flip the two numbers because of the commutative property of multiplication. In the case of this problem that is not a word problem, flipping them would give me the same answer. In a word problem, flipping them might get me the wrong answer.
2. My next step is to multiply the number in the ones place of the bottom number (3) by the number in the ones place of the top number (2) to get 6. 3 × 2 = 6.	32 × 23 96	This is a pretty simple two-digit × two-digit problem because all the products are one-digit numbers. I do not need to worry about carrying.

(continued on next page)

Figure 2.1: Worked Example of Double-Digit Multiplication With Sample Student Script and Self-Reflections *(continued)*

Student Script for the Worked Example	Worked Example	Self-Reflections
3. The next step is to write a 0 in the units column below the first product. It looks like this. I do this because my next step will be to multiply the two numbers in the tens columns: 3 and 2.	32 x 23 — 96 0	Putting that 0 in place is important so I do not forget that my next set of numbers will be in the tens column.
4. Now I am going to multiply the number in the tens place of the bottom number (2) by 2 in the ones place of the top number (2 × 2 = 4) and write the 4 below the 9 left of the zero. Then I am going to multiply the number in the tens place of the bottom number (2) by the 3 in the tens place of the top number (2 × 3 = 6). Then I'm going to write that 6 to the left of the 4.	32 x 23 — 96 640	Once again, this problem is pretty simple. I do not need to do any carrying.
5. The last thing I am going to do is add up the two products (96 + 640). There is one important thing I must do that I have not had to before in this multiplication problem, and that is to remember when I add the 9 and the 4 in the tens columns, I will have to carry the 1 over the 6, making my answer 736. I could have written the number I carried over the 6, but it was easy to remember it.	32 x 23 — 96 + 640 — 736	The last step had one place I needed to carry to the next column. I decided to do it in my head although I am supposed to show my work.

Elementary Nonexample of Worked Examples

The elementary nonexample teacher has prepared a similar worked example for students but provides only the mathematical calculations. He also skips the entire section of the unit that calls for students to acquire and process the conceptual knowledge they need to more readily understand to master the two-digit × two-digit multiplication algorithm. He divides students into small groups and asks them to talk their way through the worked example, but their discussions lack focus and students soon lose interest in the worked example and begin chatting about the upcoming recess period.

Secondary Example of Worked Examples

The secondary example of the worked examples technique is based on the following learning target: *read closely to determine what the text says explicitly and make logical inferences from it; cite specific textual evidence when writing or speaking to support conclusions drawn from the text* (CCR Anchor Standard for Reading in Grades 6–12, Standard 1). The example illustrates how a secondary teacher uses a worked example to demonstrate how to execute the process in the anchor standard. The example is divided into two sections: 1) a sample template that will enable you to grasp the prerequisite lesson steps that must be in place before practice and 2) a classroom scenario describing the specific aspect of the lesson devoted to practice using the worked example.

Sample Lesson Template for Implementing Worked Examples: Grades 6–12 ELA

Table 2.3 is a sample lesson template for the secondary example. This table describes the steps in teaching the conceptual knowledge that is the basis for the skill stated in the learning target.

Table 2.3: Sample Lesson Template for Implementing Worked Examples: Grades 6–12 ELA

Teach the Conceptual Knowledge as the Basis for Acquiring the Skill, Strategy, or Process	
Implementation	Explanatory Notes for the Teacher
1. Select the learning target for your worked example.	The learning target is *read closely to determine what the text says explicitly and make logical inferences from it; cite specific textual evidence when writing or speaking to support conclusions drawn from the text* (CCR Anchor Standard for Reading in Grades 6–12, Standard 1).
2. Identify the critical content you will initially teach your students prior to introducing the worked example.	Students will understand the key concepts and vocabulary necessary to master the process: what a conclusion is, what the steps are to drawing a conclusion, what evidence is, and how evidence is needed to support a conclusion.
3. Give your students opportunities to process the important conceptual knowledge they will need to fully benefit from the worked example.	Students will process this critical content by considering how they generally reach conclusions about things: how they use evidence to draw conclusions in their own lives.
4. Develop the worked example you plan to use.	The worked example is based on a short piece of text students have previously read for another type of assignment. Figure 2.2 is the sample text.
5. Chunk the worked example into meaningful parts, and develop a set of prompts to use with students.	The text has been chunked into three chunks for ease of reading. However, ask students to draw conclusions about the text as a whole.
6. Develop a model script or anchor chart to demonstrate for students how to talk to themselves or think aloud about the various steps in the task or problem.	Figure 2.3 enumerates the steps for drawing a conclusion, and Figure 2.4 contains a model for drawing a conclusion about the sample text.

Figure 2.2 is a sample text that has been divided into three chunks for easier reading. The teacher will model drawing a conclusion about the entire text.

Figure 2.2: Sample Text

Chunk #1

I often wander around in the desert by myself and have been very fortunate in seeing lots of wildlife and in observing many of the miracles that happen every day in nature. One of my favorite memories is of an encounter with Coyote.

Chunk #2

I was walking up a lushly vegetated wash at dawn one summer morning. A coyote started ambling across the wash, then suddenly realized I was there. He began to trot away, so I sat down on the sand. That immediately aroused his interest since it's not a typical reaction from people, and it's also a very non-threatening gesture. So the coyote stopped and sat down, watching me. I simply sat, waiting for him to make the next move. He did. He lay down and put his head on his paws, still watching and assessing me. I lay down resting my head on my hands staring into those intelligent brown eyes. After a minute he rolled on his side, so of course I did too. We spent several wonderful minutes changing positions and rolling around.

Chunk #3

Suddenly Coyote sat up cocking his ears around. He glanced at me one last time as if to say goodbye, then moved off into the brush, just before a horseback rider came into view down the wash. It was an incredible, magical feeling staring into the soul of Coyote and finding myself judged worthy of a few private moments of play.

Source: Merlin, P. © 2000. Reprinted by permission of the Arizona-Sonora Desert Museum, from *A Natural History of the Sonoran Desert.*

Figure 2.3: Steps for Drawing a Conclusion

1. Read the entire text. While reading begin to ask yourself: What important decisions can I make based on the evidence? A conclusion is an important decision the reader makes about the information in the text by identifying and connecting the explicit evidence in the text.
2. Make a list of the important evidence used to support the central idea of the text.
3. Identify and connect the most important and relevant evidence.
4. Make a decision (draw a conclusion) about what the evidence means about the people, events, or ideas in the text.

Reprinted with permission from McEwan-Adkins & Burnett (2012). *20 Literacy Strategies.* Solution Tree Press.

Figure 2.4: Sample Response Including Evidence

Conclusion About the Whole Text
The author's "magical" encounter with the coyote is safe and successful because he applies his knowledge about wildlife as he interacts with the animal.
Evidence
Often wanders alone in the desert.
Observes the miracles every day.
Knows the difference between threatening and nonthreatening movements when animals are present.

Secondary Nonexample of Using Worked Examples

The secondary nonexample teacher is working with her students on the same learning target but is hesitant to devote the kind of time and energy required to develop worked examples. She feels that she does not have time to spend on laying the conceptual foundation. Furthermore, she is reluctant to present herself as a model to students when she feels that she does not write well. She gives her students the handouts that the example teacher has prepared, puts the students in groups to work through them, and assigns writing a conclusion from an article in one of the classroom readers. Her students miss several opportunities to become proficient in drawing conclusions from text based on evidence.

Determining If Students Are Proficient in Using Worked Examples

You will only know whether your students have gained proficiency in executing a skill, strategy, or process as a result of them using worked examples in their practice if they can do one or more of the following:

- execute the skill, strategy, or process as modeled in the worked example

- develop a worked example to share with a partner

- describe the steps in the skill, strategy, or process

- explain how using the worked example helps to clarify and solidify the process for them

Use the student proficiency scale in Table 2.4 to determine how well your students are progressiniig to the desired result when practicing using worked examples.

Table 2.4: Student Proficiency Scale for Practicing Skills, Strategies, and Processes Using Worked Examples

Emerging	Fundamental	Desired Result
Students can identify the skill, strategy, or process in a worked example.	Students can explain the key steps in the skill, strategy, or process in a worked example.	Students can explain how they used the skill, strategy, or process to work the example.
Students can identify a worked example involving a specific skill, strategy, or process.	Students can identify key steps necessary in a worked example involving a specific skill, strategy, or process.	Students can develop a worked example involving a specific skill, strategy, or process.
Students are able to replicate the work in the worked example.	Students use the worked example to guide them as they solve other problems and evaluate their own performance.	Students use the skill, strategy, or process to solve other problems and evaluate their own performance.
Students can identify parts of the worked example that helped them learn.	Students can explain how the worked example helped them learn the skill, strategy, or process.	Students can specifically explain how using the worked example helped clarify and deepen their understanding of the skill, strategy, or process.

Scaffold and Extend Instruction to Meet Students' Need

As you become more skilled in using worked examples for practice activities, you will find that you can more readily identify individuals or small groups of students who need something more or different from the original instruction. Some students need support, or scaffolding, that takes them from where they are to where they need to be. Other students need to be challenged by extending the ways in which you expect them to interact with worked examples. Use the following suggestions as springboards for zeroing in on the needs of your students.

Scaffolding

When students are having difficulty following the student scripts or worked examples here are some ways to adjust your instruction:

- Write the student script in more student-friendly language.

- Provide more visual cues to help students understand the steps of a worked example.

- Chunk the worked example into smaller parts so students become comfortable with one step before leading them to another.

Extending

For some students, you may need to go beyond what you have assigned to the rest of the class. Try these ideas for extending worked examples:

- Assign students to develop worked examples for various types of student learners.

- Assign students to develop easier worked examples of students who need more support.

- Assign students to develop worked examples in other formats: video, PPT, or audio.

Instructional Technique 3

FREQUENT STRUCTURED PRACTICE

Frequent structured practice is practice scheduled at specific intervals and guided by a coach or teacher during the initial stages of learning. This type of practice is also referred to as *massed practice*. Coupled with the close monitoring technique introduced previously, practice that is both highly structured and occurs frequently is the most efficient practice technique to help students acquire new procedural knowledge.

During the introduction of a new skill, the learner needs to hear a think-aloud or see a demonstration of a skill, strategy, or process. Once the actions of the skill, strategy, or process are visible, the learner needs time to try it out with the support of a teacher. Using well-designed tasks that move from simple to complex ensures that learners can successfully execute the new skill. The frequency and structure of the practice sessions provide a format for teachers to monitor that students are accurately acquiring critical content and developing automaticity. Typically, three to five highly structured practice sessions spaced closely together, with a teacher providing prompting and feedback, will enable many learners to achieve the level of mastery needed to move on to more varied and independent practice. Some students may need greater amounts of frequent structured practice.

How to Effectively Implement Frequent Structured Practice

The effective implementation of frequent structured practice begins with planning for the types of practice your students need. Allocate no more than thirty minutes or less for your frequent structured practice sessions. Within approximately twenty-four hours of the initial learning, learners should have another opportunity for a highly structured practice session. These sessions will ideally continue over the next couple of days, or in the case of more complex skills, weeks, until students are able to successfully execute the skill without your guided practice. Gradually, more complex tasks are introduced and practice may become less structured and frequent. At that point, students will be ready to transition to fluency building and eventually to more challenging varied practice sessions.

Table 3.1 contains a sample lesson template for the steps leading up to the structured practice session as well as more detailed information about what actually transpires during a frequent structured practice session. One of the key steps in any practice session is the point at which you explicitly demonstrate or think aloud about a new skill, strategy, or process. Following the demonstration, students are given a similar task containing content that is easily understood and requires the students to focus their thinking on the successful performance of the skill, strategy, or process. Recall from the close monitoring technique that it is more effective to give students easier tasks at the outset. As students perform the task, questions are posed to guide students' thinking. Correct application of the skill is immediately reinforced, and incorrect usage is quickly identified so adjustments can be made. At the end of each practice session, students reflect on their learning progress.

The greatest temptation when planning for frequent structured practice is to short-cut the instruction of the essential conceptual knowledge that serves as the foundation for students' understanding at the same time they are practicing it to fluency. Without the prerequisite concepts in mind, students' practice can be reduced to rote memorization of meaningless steps or total confusion and frustration. When practice or homework assignments unravel, the first place to look for an answer is in Part 1 of the lesson template—teaching the conceptual knowledge that is inherent in the skill, strategy, or process. Part 1 of the template cannot be folded into tight timelines. The steps might cover several days or even a much longer period of time. Once you are satisfied that your students are ready, move to Part 2 of the template—designing the practice session. Part 3 of the template describes the actual practice task—what students will do to include several accurate executions of the skill.

Table 3.1: Sample Lesson Template for Effectively Implementing Frequent Structured Practice

PART 1: Teach the Conceptual Knowledge That Is Inherent in the Skill, Strategy, or Process	
Implementation	Explanatory Notes for the Teacher
1. Select the learning target for your frequent structured practice.	You cannot implement frequent structured practice if you have not identified the skill, strategy, or process you want students to learn.
2. Identify the critical content you will initially teach your students prior to introducing the skill, strategy, or process.	Identifying the conceptual knowledge that is inherent in the skill you want students to master is essential. If students do not understand key concepts or vocabulary, your modeling and their practice can become rote repetition rather than the acquisition of critical content.
3. Identify the ways in which you will have your students process this critical content, and give students opportunities to process the important conceptual knowledge they will need to fully benefit from the practice sessions.	Provide content materials at students independent reading levels.
PART 2: Do Before Your Practice Session	
1. Determine how you will monitor students' performance of the skill, strategy, or process.	Frequent structured practice is a type of guided practice that will be sustained over several days or weeks, depending on the complexity of the skill or process. Initially it requires the type of close monitoring described in Technique 1 that enables you to correct an error, ask a guiding question, or point students in a more productive direction. Small groups are the most productive way to implement frequent structured practice.
2. Determine how you will chunk the skill, strategy, or process to make it more manageable.	Begin with a smaller chunk or step of the skill, strategy, or process to give your students a greater likelihood of experiencing immediate success during their first practice session.

(continued on next page)

Table 3.1: Sample Lesson Template for Effectively Implementing Frequent Structured Practice *(continued)*

PART 2: Do Before Your Practice Session *(continued)*	
3. If appropriate for the skill, strategy, or process and for the grade and content, prepare an anchor chart that gives students visual cues for reviewing the steps of a skill, strategy, or process.	Anchor charts should include a definition or description and the steps for carrying out a multi-step skill, strategy, or process. In addition to anchor charts, consider preparing a handout for students to consult. They can use this handout during later independent practice sessions.
4. Develop a menu of guiding questions that fit with your grade level and content.	For example, while students practice a math procedure, ask the following questions: 1) How should you begin? 2) What do you need to do next? 3) How will you check your work?
PART 3: Practice the Skill, Strategy, or Process	
1. Select the practice task that students will execute.	If the skill is complex, break it into smaller, more manageable chunks. Connect the practice task to the learning target as well as the desired results you want to see from your students.
2. Explicitly demonstrate and think aloud regarding the skill, strategy, or process you want students to practice during the session.	Take care to make the demonstration or think-aloud clear and explicit. Think of ways to make your thinking as visible as possible to students.
3. Observe students practicing the task.	Take anecdotal notes, if appropriate. Coach, prompt, and praise students. Ensure that all students are responding. Do not use round robin or turn-taking activities for frequent structured practice sessions.
4. Debrief the practice session.	Ask students to explain how they used the skill, strategy, or process or what they were thinking as they executed the practice task.

Common Mistakes

There are several ways a teacher can fail to maximize the desired effects of frequent structured practice:

- The teacher fails to lay a foundation for successful practice by not teaching the essential conceptual knowledge.

- The teacher fails to communicate to students exactly what they are practicing and why.

- The teacher fails to review the steps of a skill, strategy, or process.

- The teacher fails to adequately demonstrate or model the skill, strategy, or process.

- The teacher attempts to teach and practice a skill that is too difficult for the students' present levels of understanding.

- The teacher fails to closely monitor students' errors and immediately correct them by modeling or demonstrating a correct model.

- The teacher fails to build in opportunities for every student to practice the skill, strategy, or process.

- The teacher does not provide adequate amounts of structure to the practice session, thereby losing the attention and focus of students.

Examples and Nonexamples of Frequent Structured Practice

As you consider these examples and nonexamples of frequent structured practice, read carefully to identify the common mistakes, and pay close attention to the suggestions for how to effectively implement frequent structured practice.

Elementary Example of Frequent Structured Practice

The example demonstrates how an elementary teacher develops and conducts a structured practice session during reading instruction. The learning target for this elementary example is *asking and answering questions about key details in a text* (CCSS.ELA-Literacy.RI.1.1). Her first practice session will be followed by one or two additional practice sessions to give students opportunities to acquire the critical content. The example is divided into two sections: 1) a sample lesson that will enable you to understand the flow of the lesson and 2) a classroom scenario describing the same lesson.

A Sample Lesson for Implementing Frequent Structured Practice: First-Grade Literacy

Table 3.2 provides a completed lesson template that corresponds to the following classroom scenario. Parts 1 and 2 of the template will help you understand what happened in the classroom scenario prior to the practice session. Only the actual practice session will be in the classroom scenario that follows.

Table 3.2: Sample Lesson Template for Implementing Frequent Structured Practice: First-Grade Literacy

PART 1: Teach the Conceptual Knowledge That Is Inherent in the Skill, Strategy, or Process	
Implementation	Explanatory Notes for the Teacher
1. Select the learning target for your frequent structured practice.	The learning target for this example is *asking and answering questions about key details in a text* (CCSS.ELA-Literacy.RI.1.1).
2. Identify the critical content you will initially teach your students prior to introducing the skill, strategy, or process.	The teacher has taught students what details are, showing and reading aloud to them both examples and nonexamples from various texts. The teacher has also taught the concept of questioning and the difference between asking a question and answering a question. She frequently refers to and uses these concepts during the school day in other lessons.
3. Identify the ways in which you will have your students process this critical content, and give students opportunities to process the important declarative (conceptual) knowledge they will need to fully benefit from the practice sessions.	To help her students process this background knowledge more fully, the teacher often takes time during the reading of stories to read aloud a short phrase and ask students if that would be a key detail or a *trivial* detail (a grown-up word her students love to use). She has taught the question words—who, what, where, when, why, and how—to prompt good questions. Students are not limited to using these question words, but they are helpful for students who cannot figure out how to get started asking a question.
PART 2: Practice the Skill, Strategy, or Process	
1. Select the practice task students will execute.	The practice task students will execute in this session is asking the author of the book questions about the book after they have reviewed all aspects of the book (cover, title, back cover copy, illustrations, etc.). The teacher writes down the questions they generate on her whiteboard. Students will then read the text together to find key details that answer their questions.

2. Explicitly demonstrate and think aloud regarding the skill, strategy, or process you want students to practice during the session.	The teacher models asking the author a question and reading to find a key detail that will answer the question. She reminds students that not every question they ask will be answered in the text. They may need to find answers in other places. She reminds them of the question words they can use and points out an anchor chart in the classroom to scaffold their questioning technique.
3. Observe students practicing the task.	Take anecdotal notes about students' progress with the skill. Make notes about how to structure the follow-up structured practice.
4. Debrief the practice session.	Students participate in a brief discussion by explaining what they were thinking as they used the "ask the author"–read–find a key detail to answer the question process.

Classroom Scenario for Implementing Frequent Structured Practice

Our example teacher has laid a solid foundation of conceptual knowledge with her students prior to this practice session. Students have their own copies of a somewhat easy-to-read science book titled *From Caterpillar to Butterfly* by Deborah Heiligman (1996). They have previously heard the book read aloud as part of a science unit, but today they will use the text in a practice activity called *ask the author*. The students will generate questions to ask the author based on inferences they have made about the book by looking at its cover, considering what the title means, flipping through the pages to check out the illustrations, and reading the back cover copy to try to find key details the author has provided in the new text they are reading together and use them to answer and generate questions about the details. Then, they will read to find details that answer the questions they asked the author.

Here is how the teacher introduces the session to her students:

> Boys and girls, today we are going to ask the author of this book some questions and see if we can find details in the book that answer those questions. Remember that when we ask the author questions, we are really asking questions that we would like to know the answers to. The only way we can

get answers to our questions from the author is to carefully read the words the author has written in the book. Yesterday during science class, before we read this book for the first time, we made a list of questions we thought might be answered in the book. Today we are going to read again more carefully to see if we can pick out details in the book that answer our questions.

The teacher hangs up the chart paper on which she recorded the questions the class had previously generated. Here are some of their questions:

- Where did the caterpillar come from?

- How long does it take a caterpillar to get big enough?

- What do caterpillars eat?

- Why did you write a book about butterflies?

- Who drew the pictures of all the beautiful butterflies in the book?

- How long does the caterpillar stay in the little house he makes?

- What do you call that little house?

- How can an ugly caterpillar turn into something so beautiful?

First, I want to show you how we are going to find details in the book that answer the questions we wrote down. I am going to read the first page and pay close attention to the important details.

The teacher reads the first page: "Today a caterpillar came to school in a jar. It is eating green leaves. It is climbing and wiggling. This tiny caterpillar is going to change. It will change into a beautiful butterfly" *(Heiligman, 1996, p. 5).*

I've finished reading the page, and now I'm going to go back to the board and read over the questions we asked to see if there's a detail in the book that will answer one of those questions. *The teacher reads the questions aloud until she comes to the question:* What do caterpillars eat? *She glances at the first page of the book again and explains that she has found a detail in the book that answers the question. She directs students to look at the page with her. The important detail is:* It is eating green leaves.

Boys and girls, we're going to chorally read each page, and I want you to think about the questions we have written to see if you can find a detail on the page that answers that question.

Let's begin reading together. All eyes on the first word on the next page. "Caterpillars usually turn into butterflies outdoors. They live in gardens, and meadows and yards. But we will watch our caterpillar change into a butterfly right here in our classroom. This change is called metamorphosis." Turn to your partner and together find the question you asked the author and read the sentence that gives the details.

The teacher guides the students in reading about halfway through the book and finding details that answer their questions. She wraps up the session this way:

Class you have done some excellent work. You asked the author very good questions yesterday and today you have found answers to several of those questions by finding key details in the book that answered them. Tomorrow we're going to ask, read, and answer again. I think you are becoming expert readers and thinkers.

Elementary Nonexample of Frequent Structured Practice

The nonexample teacher attempts to plan structured practice for her students but tries to do everything at once. Rather than laying a solid foundation of conceptual knowledge and scaffolding students' reading of the text so they can concentrate on comprehension, she develops the questions and then assigns students to work with their partners to find the answers to the questions. She fails to focus on the concept of details and why they are critical to successfully getting explicit meaning from the text. The practice session ends abruptly when two students begin to argue with the rest of the group about their answers.

Secondary Example of Frequent Structured Practice

This secondary example demonstrates how a tenth-grade history teacher develops a structured practice session with his students. The example is divided into two sections: 1) a completed lesson template that will enable you to grasp the flow of the lesson and 2) a classroom scenario describing the same lesson. Recall from the elementary lesson the necessity for laying a conceptual foundation before planning to practice a skill, strategy, or process.

A Sample Template for Effectively Implementing Frequent Structured Practice: Tenth-Grade History

Table 3.3 describes a tenth-grade history lesson using frequent structured practice.

Table 3.3: Sample Lesson Template for Implementing Frequent Structured Practice: Tenth-Grade History

PART 1: Teach the Conceptual Knowledge That Is Inherent in the Skill, Strategy, or Process	
Implementation	Explanatory Notes for the Teacher
1. Select the learning target for your frequent structured practice.	The learning target for this secondary example is *determine the meaning of words and phrases as they are used in a text, including vocabulary describing political, social, or economic aspects of history/social studies* (CCSS Literacy in History/Social Studies, Science, and Technical Studies, Reading 6–12, Standard 4 specifically for Grades 9–10).

2. Identify the critical content you will initially teach your students prior to introducing the skill, strategy, or process.	The English teacher has taught students a strategy for interpreting words and phrases and how an author's words help us visualize and connect with the feelings of a specific event or emotion. The strategy steps are in an anchor chart on the classroom wall and can be found in Figure 3.1.
3. Identify the ways in which you will have your students process this critical content, and give students opportunities to process the important declarative (conceptual) knowledge they will need to fully benefit from the practice sessions.	Students have been closely reading primary and secondary accounts of historical explorations. The teacher has been pointing out new words that may be unfamiliar in the context of the modern world. He now wants students to practice using the historical setting and contextual situation as a strategy for interpreting meanings of the words and phrases encountered in these texts.
PART 2: Practice the Skill, Strategy, or Process	
1. Select the practice task that students will execute.	The practice task that students will execute in is using the historical setting and contextual situations for interpreting meanings of the words and phrases they encounter in these texts. The teacher has modeled this strategy using the anchor chart a number of times for students, but he wants them to have more structured practice.
2. Explicitly demonstrate and think aloud regarding the skill, strategy, or process you want students to practice during the session.	He first specifically models the strategy using a word he has selected from *The Longitude Prize* by Joan Dash (2000), a book the class has been reading. He refers to the anchor chart and brings his knowledge of the historical setting to figuring out the meaning of the words in their context.
3. Observe students practicing the task.	The teacher listens to how students are using the anchor chart. He knows they will need additional practice.
4. Debrief the practice session.	Students reflect on how using the anchor chart helps them interpret the words from the text.

The anchor chart in Figure 3.1 is similar to the one the teacher prepared. You can post this chart on the wall or provide as a handout to students to place in their academic notebooks for reference.

Figure 3.1: Anchor Chart: Figuring Out What Words and Phrases Mean

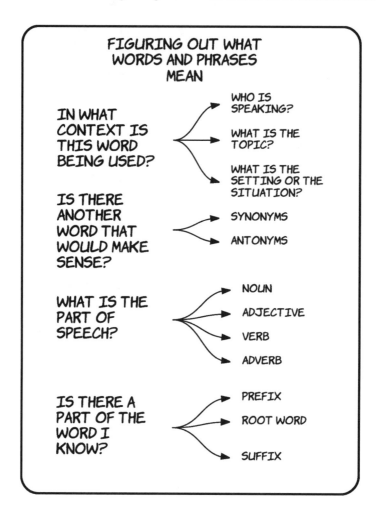

Classroom Scenario for Implementing Frequent Structured Practice: Tenth-Grade History

The secondary example teacher has designed a unit on exploration in the 17th and 18th centuries. Students are practicing this skill during their reading of an excerpt from *The Longitude Prize* by Joan Dash (2000). Here is how he introduces his lesson:

Class, as I read historical accounts I often come across words that are unfamiliar to me. I know that your English teacher has developed an anchor chart showing you ways to figure out the meanings of terms that often seem strange to us but had meaning centuries ago. We will go back into the text and examine the words and phrases that Joan Dash uses in chapter 1 of **The Longitude Prize** to see if we can get a deeper sense of the historical setting and emotions of the explorers described in the excerpt. Please reread and circle any words that are either new to you or are used in interesting ways. *Students read silently and circle words they do not know.* Now that you've revisited this first excerpt, work with your talking partner to share the words you circled. I want to hear you discuss what you are thinking as you interpreted the meanings of the words. You can refer to the anchor chart to figure out what words and phrases mean. *As students work with their partner, the teacher closely monitors, taking note of when students are and are not using the guiding questions. After three minutes, the teacher calls time and debriefs the content.* So how did thinking about the time period of this text and the situation help you interpret the word **reckoning**? What is the topic of this excerpt? What words are related to the topic? How is the narrator feeling? How does understanding the feelings of the narrator help you interpret words or phrases? *The teacher asks students to read and discuss the next excerpt. This continues for several chunks of the text. At the end of the activity, he asks students to debrief the process of using the four questions on the anchor chart to interpret the word meaning.* How does this process help you interpret the word meanings? How does this process help you understand the author's message? Why is it important to think about the historical setting and topic to interpret new words or phrases? Remember, our goal is to automatically interpret words and phrases as we read primary and secondary sources.

Secondary Nonexample of Frequent Structured Practice

In the history class across the hall, the students are reading the same text containing a primary and secondary source. However, the teacher does not provide the students with a process of reading historical accounts or how to interpret words and phrases. Students are reading the next section of the text, taking turns reading out loud. About 30 percent of the class is engaged in listening to the text and actively participating in the conversation. The teacher is randomly calling on students. Most students are not able to discuss word meanings or describe the context provided as a way to interpreting the meanings, because the practice is not focused on a strategy to use during reading for meaning. As a result of this activity, some students will have encountered new declarative knowledge, but in a few days, weeks, or months, this day will long be forgotten. Because this instruction is focused on a text, rather than how to think and process the text and others like it, the students will not transfer skills, strategies, and processes needed to be college and career ready.

Determining If Students Are Proficient in Using Frequent Structured Practice

Students respond to practice problems, skill practices, and process exercises using miniboards to respond while the teacher scans responses and clarifies as needed to ensure continued success with similar problems, practices, or exercises. Make sure of the following:

- Students pair with a partner and quietly explain a concept or process to each other while you circulate and listen.

- Students write their answers to questions or problems in their academic notebooks.

The student proficiency scale for the effectiveness of frequent structured practice activities is in Table 3.4. It will help you assess how well your students are benefiting from the types of practice activities you are using. Use the scale to help you monitor for the desired result of your students' frequent structured practice.

Table 3.4: Student Proficiency Scale for Practicing Skills, Strategies, and Processes Using Frequent Structured Practice

Emerging	Fundamental	Desired Result
Students can restate some of the steps or components of the skill, strategy, or process.	When explaining the skill, strategy, or process, parts are missed or incorrectly stated.	As a result of frequent structured practice, students can explain the steps of the skill, strategy, or process.
With teacher prompting, the student can perform the skill, strategy, or process.	Students are able to execute the skill, strategy, or process, but some errors or misunderstandings still exist.	Student can show the steps of the skill, strategy, or process by modeling or using pictures or drawings. Students have no misunderstandings or errors in thinking as they perform the skill, strategy, or process.

Scaffold and Extend Instruction to Meet Students' Needs

The ways in which you scaffold and extend practice activities will depend on your grade level and content. Here are some examples of how to meet the needs of students who need extra support as well as examples for extending the learning of more accelerated students.

Scaffolding

- Show students a video, give them a wordless book, or have them listen and follow along with a recording of the text. You will need to set "stop and think" points for these students to cue them to perform the strategy, skill, or process.

- Provide independent or instructional-level problems or texts for each student. If the goal is for the students to understand and use a strategy, skill, or process, you should accomplish this with simpler problems or texts.

- Provide students with concrete objects or manipulatives to use in solving a problem.

- Use drawings or symbols to scaffold students' understanding of text.

Extending

- Expect students to read more challenging texts or solve more complex problems.

- Ask students to track their progress with a skill, strategy, or process to determine when they are ready to move to varied practice.

- In some situations, students will benefit from becoming tutors or coaches for students needing additional support. Provide tutors with bookmarks or anchor charts with the practice structure to be used.

PART II

INDEPENDENT PRACTICE

There are three independent practice techniques in Part II. During independent practice activities, students are expected to take more ownership regarding the application of procedural knowledge during the execution of increasingly rigorous tasks and problems.

Instructional Technique 4

FLUENCY PRACTICE

Fluency is the development of a skill, strategy, or process to one of two levels: automatic processing or controlled processing. Automatic processing is characterized by automaticity and speed. When students are automatically able to execute a skill, strategy, or process with no conscious thought or attention to what they are doing, their working memories are free for other cognitive tasks—comprehending what they are reading or executing more complex mathematical algorithms with no hesitation.

Controlled processing is the goal for more complex processes such as writing an essay or designing a scientific experiment. Controlled processing means that learners must consciously attend to the various steps or aspects of the required process to execute it, while also attending to the specifics of the assignment and giving thought as to how best to complete the task. As learners mature and become more expert, processes that once required more controlled processing can often become more automatic. However, the achievement of fluency, whether automatic *or* controlled, requires practice—multiple executions of the skill or process.

How to Effectively Implement Fluency Practice

At every grade level and in every content area, there are skills, strategies, and processes that need to be developed to fluency, whether automatic or controlled. The effective implementation of fluency practice depends on your identification of both the critical content of your grade level that requires automatic processing as well as that requires controlled processing.

Implementation of Practice for Skills That Require Automatic Processing

The two most critical skills that students need to practice to automaticity are word reading and single-digit multiplication. Both of these skill sets are based on concepts that students must understand to achieve success in school and beyond. However, in the case of fluency in both word reading and single-digit multiplication, these conceptual understandings must be combined with intensive practice. Undoubtedly some students or groups of students need far more practice than others, but without a combination of both conceptual understanding and fluency, students will be unable to apply their reading and mathematics knowledge at increasingly rigorous levels and do so with automaticity.

Word Reading Fluency

The key to word reading fluency is reading a lot. The optimum period for building word reading fluency is in grades 1–2. However, before the majority of students can read a lot, they need to acquire basic conceptual knowledge about the reading process, experience daily positive experiences with literacy, and be directly and explicitly instructed in the basic reading skills, to include: 1) sounding out regular words—first orally, then subvocally, and finally quickly; 2) reading irregular (sometimes called *exception* or *sight*) words that cannot be decoded and must be memorized; and 3) reading advanced words using conceptual knowledge about prefixes and suffixes and how to divide words into syllables.

There will always be a certain group of students who have developed word reading fluency on their own prior to entering school. These students have likely been reading a lot independently and will not need your help with word reading fluency. These students will continue to read a lot. They have become voracious readers on their own. There are some students who have acquired the aforementioned skills at some point but have failed to develop fluency because they did not get enough practice reading a lot at their independent reading level. There are still others who have failed to develop fluency because they did not have any direct and explicit instruction in word reading skills. Table 4.1 enumerates the steps in building word reading fluency. You will immediately notice that designing practice for building word reading fluency is somewhat different from designing practice for discrete skills. It requires a more global and constant daily practice in the classroom and at home.

The goal of building word reading fluency is to develop confident, thoughtful readers with strong vocabularies and excellent comprehension, *not* speed-readers.

Table 4.1: Steps for Building Word Reading Fluency

Implementation	Explanatory Notes for the Teacher
1. Provide a classroom environment filled with a library of expository and narrative texts at a variety of reading levels.	The goal is to have the right book at the right moment for a child to read independently. If you expect students to read books with words they cannot independently read, they will become frustrated and fall behind.
2. Build an excitement about books and learning that leads students to a desire to learn to read on their own.	Reading aloud to students does not build word reading fluency. However, it builds vocabulary and background knowledge and a motivation to acquire word reading independence.
3. Explicitly teach the basic skills of reading, and as quickly as possible engage students in the oral reading of text at their independent reading levels.	Students who have acquired the sound–spelling correspondences of several consonants and one or two vowels can soon fluently read words.
4. Provide daily oral reading practice in accessible text for every student. Accessible text is text at students' independent reading levels.	Devote up to forty-five minutes per day for students' independent reading. You can divide the time period into shorter segments that feature different types of activities. There is no substitute for wide reading if you want to build fluency.
5. Build comprehension, endurance, and accountability in your read-a-lot periods.	One-minute reading probes may be helpful for assessing students' reading fluency, but they can also have unintended consequences. Some students may fail to get any meaning from reading such a short passage. Students may begin to associate the act of reading with speed instead of meaning, creating bad habits.
6. Organize an at-home reading component of thirty minutes per day.	Send home book bags with books at students' independent reading levels to read aloud to parents or caregivers.
7. Facilitate fluency building in your guided reading groups by using a variety of oral reading methods.	Rasinski et al. (1994) suggest a combination of reading aloud, choral reading, listening to students read, and reading performance you should implement over a period of days. Students listen to you read a poem or other text to the class. They read the text chorally, then pair and practice reading the text with a classmate, and finally perform for an audience—either another class at their grade level or a class of younger or older students.

(continued on next page)

Table 4.1: Steps for Building Word Reading Fluency *(continued)*

Implementation	Explanatory Notes for the Teacher
8. Have students keep track of the books they read and set personal reading goals in a reading journal.	At the beginning of the school year, the books students can read independently will be at easy reading levels, but reading a lot will guarantee that students can progress to more difficult reading levels. Monitor students' progress carefully and motivate them to read increasingly more challenging texts.

Adapted from McEwan (2009) and McEwan-Adkins (2010).

Single-Digit Multiplication Fluency

Developing speed and accuracy in the core function of single-digit multiplication is essential for all students. However, as with word reading fluency, developing multiplication fluency must occur simultaneously with the acquisition of key concepts by using manipulatives and hands-on activities. You will know your students are ready to begin working on fluency when they understand the process of multiplication and can use successive addition or manipulatives to figure out their answers. At that point, they should begin practicing single-digit multiplication to fluency. However, transitioning students from the acquisition of concepts to automatic processing is often a stumbling block for teachers.

In desperation, some teachers resort to weekly timed tests with one hundred problems that overwhelm and frustrate students. These types of tests are quite justifiably described as "drill and kill." Other teachers, anxious to move on to complex algorithms, give up completely and provide students with a multiplication chart that has all the answers arranged in a grid or pass out the calculators. Still others hand off the responsibility to parents, who are no more successful than teachers have been. For the students at that point, the mental and physical effort required to find correct answers on the chart or use a calculator interferes with developing fluency in executing algorithms like multiplying double-digit numerals, long division, or the division of fractions.

The following components are crucial to developing fluency: 1) a specific performance criterion for introducing new problems (e.g., complete mastery of a previous small set of facts), 2) intensive practice on newly introduced problems (two one-and-one-half-minute oral repetitions of each new problem four times), 3) systematic practice on previously introduced problems, 4) adequate time allotted for daily practice, 5) a recordkeeping system, and 6) a motivation system (Stein, Silbert & Carnine, 1997). Table 4.2 provides an overview of the steps involved in the effective implementation of building fluency in single-digit multiplication. Once you are familiar with the structural features of a practice program, Table 4.3 describes what the actual practice looks like.

Table 4.2: Steps for Building Single-Digit Multiplication Fluency

Implementation	Explanatory Notes for the Teacher
1. If you are developing fluency practice for an entire lower-grade-level class (third or fourth grade), pair students and begin the practice regimen for all students with the same set of four problems (one set of two problems and their reversals; for example, 3 × 5 and 5 × 3; and 5 × 6 and 6 × 5). Gradually add additional sets of problems four at a time.	Students may need to be regrouped as their automaticity levels spread out. At that point, pair students according to the similarity of their fluency levels. Partners who are at or about the same fluency level will work together more smoothly than partners with varied processing speeds. They may even develop a sense of competitiveness that motivates them.
2. If you are developing fluency practice for a small group of students, first determine their levels of automaticity. Build your practice sets around problems they have not mastered. Pair students with similar levels of automaticity.	Automaticity means that students can give the answers without hesitation after reading a problem aloud, such as "7 × 8 is 56," or give an answer to a problem that is read aloud within a second.
3. Practice with small sets of problems, two to four at a time. Students must remember the answers rather than derive them from previous knowledge. Students may attempt to use a learned strategy or shortcut, but explain that they must answer in a second or less. The four problems should be a set of two problems and their reversals (5 × 8 and 8 × 5) and (6 × 9 and 9 × 6).	Practice to automaticity (immediate recall) with a small set of problems before you introduce more. Students can achieve fluency far more quickly if they practice to master a small set of problems.
4. Begin with the more difficult problems, such as 3 × 8, 4 × 7, 6 × 9, and 6 × 7, and do not move on until students master the first set.	Timed tests are essential, but they are only given over facts that have already been mastered. Success is achieved in small increments. Build in a parent component for the new sets of problems. However, if you want to enlist parents, hold a small training session for them, showing them what practice should look like.
5. Develop a record-keeping system and build a structure to motivate students.	Students will be more motivated if they can chart their progress in small increments and see an upward trajectory on their line graphs.

Adapted from Stein, Silbert & Carnine (1997) and Crawford (2015).

To develop practice worksheets, select problems students have not mastered and then gradually recycle previously introduced and mastered problems back into the mix. Table 4.3 describes the steps in the actual practice sequence.

Table 4.3: Steps in a Sample Single-Digit Multiplication Practice Sequence

Implementation	Explanatory Notes for the Teacher
1. Give two students a practice worksheet divided into two parts. The top half of the sheet provides practice on newly introduced problems and from the two preceding sets of problems. Each of the newly introduced problems appears four times. Each of the problems from the set just introduced earlier would appear three times, and each of the problems from the set that preceded that one would appear twice. The pair is also given an answer key to use during their oral practice.	Figure 4.1 illustrates a practice worksheet used after students have previously mastered two sets of two problems each. Again students practice the previously mastered problems while you introduce two new sets of problems for the first time. Figure 4.2 is the answer key for the practice sheet. Provide this to the "tutor" partner in the practice session. Figure 4.3 is a sample test form.
2. A pair of students spends ten to fifteen minutes practicing. One student orally practices, while the other student follows along with an answer key. Students practice the problems twice (three minutes of practice).	The first partner practices by stating the complete problem and answer: "5 × 7 = 35." If the student makes an error, such as "5 × 7 = 49," the tutor (the student with the answers) corrects his partner by stating the complete correct answer: "5 × 7 = 35" and asks the student to repeat the complete correct answer: "5 × 7 = 35." Students have 1½ minutes to complete this practice. They exchange the answer key, and the second student states the complete problems with answers following the established pattern. Each partner completes one practice. They exchange the answer key, and Partner 1 becomes the tutor holding the answer key while Partner 2 orally practices the problems. They exchange the answer key once more. At this point, each partner has practiced the problems twice.
3. The bottom half of the practice sheet consists of a timed one-minute test of thirty problems. Students who get twenty-eight of the thirty items correct within one minute have passed the worksheet.	As soon as students are developing fluency with orally giving answers, transition to writing the answers. As students are able to fluently say and write correct answers in one minute, increase the number of test problems to forty.

Figure 4.1 illustrates a sample practice worksheet for single-digit multiplication. Tailor your practice worksheets to the problems your students have not mastered, giving students at least four practice opportunities for each problem that has just been introduced, with problems from previously mastered sets have fewer practice opportunities.

Figure 4.1: Sample Practice Worksheet for Single-Digit Multiplication Fluency

8 × 3 =	7 × 6 =	3 × 8 =	6 × 7 =	6 × 9 =	7 × 6 =
9 × 6 =	4 × 9 =	7 × 4 =	4 × 9 =	9 × 8 =	3 × 8 =
7 × 6 =	9 × 8 =	3 × 8 =	8 × 9 =	4 × 7 =	6 × 7 =
9 × 6 =	7 × 6 =	4 × 7 =	6 × 9 =	8 × 9 =	9 × 4 =
6 × 7 =	4 × 9 =	9 × 4 =	7 × 4 =	4 × 9 =	8 × 3 =
8 × 3 =	9 × 6 =	7 × 6 =	8 × 3 =	6 × 7 =	6 × 9 =

Key to Problem Sets

1. Newly introduced problem sets: 8 × 3 =; 3 × 8 =; 6 × 7 =; and 7 × 6 =

2. Problem sets previously introduced: 9 × 6 =; 6 × 9 =; 4 × 9 =; and 9 × 4 =

3. Problem sets from the preceding set: 7 × 4 =; 4 × 7 =; 9 × 8 =; and 8 × 9 =

Figure 4.2 illustrates a sample answer sheet for the practice worksheet (36 problems) shown in Figure 4.1. The tutor (student who holds the answer sheet and monitors the accuracy of the other student's answers) is also "practicing" in a sense while listening for the right answers and correcting any errors her partner makes during the practice session.

Figure 4.2: Sample Single-Digit Multiplication Fluency Answer Sheet

8 × 3 = 24	7 × 6 = 42	3 × 8 = 24	6 × 7 = 42	6 × 9 = 54	7 × 6 = 42
9 × 6 = 54	4 × 9 = 36	7 × 4 = 28	4 × 9 = 36	9 × 8 = 72	3 × 8 = 24
7 × 6 = 42	9 × 8 = 72	3 × 8 = 24	8 × 9 = 72	4 × 7 = 28	6 × 7 = 42
9 × 6 = 54	7 × 6 = 42	4 × 7 = 28	6 × 9 = 54	8 × 9 = 72	9 × 4 = 36
6 × 7 = 42	4 × 9 = 36	9 × 4 = 36	7 × 4 = 28	4 × 9 = 36	8 × 3 = 24
8 × 3 = 24	9 × 6 = 54	7 × 6 = 42	8 × 3 = 24	6 × 7 = 42	6 × 9 = 54

Key to Problem Sets

1. Newly introduced problem sets: 8 × 3 =; 3 × 8 =; 6 × 7 =; and 7 × 6 =

2. Problem sets previously introduced: 9 × 6 =; 6 × 9 =; 4 × 9 =; and 9 × 4 =

3. Problem sets from the preceding set: 7 × 4 =; 4 × 7 =; 9 × 8 =; and 8 × 9 =

Figure 4.3 illustrates a sample test (thirty problems) over new problems on the practice sheet shown in Figure 4.1. Students must answer twenty-eight out of thirty problems correctly in under a minute to move on to a new practice sheet. Students will work with the same practice sheet during the next practice session if they do not score twenty-eight out of thirty correct. If a student pair is motivated, they can fit in extra practice sessions other times during the day.

Figure 4.3: Sample Single-Digit Multiplication Timed Test

8 × 3 =	7 × 6 =	9 × 8 =	6 × 7 =	9 × 6 =	8 × 5 =
6 × 9 =	3 × 8 =	4 × 7 =	4 × 9 =	8 × 3 =	4 × 9 =
9 × 8 =	9 × 6 =	6 × 7 =	7 × 4 =	8 × 9 =	6 × 9 =
8 × 3 =	7 × 6 =	9 × 8 =	6 × 7 =	9 × 6 =	8 × 5 =
6 × 9 =	3 × 8 =	4 × 7 =	4 × 9 =	8 × 3 =	4 × 9 =

Automatic Processing of Algorithms

Once students have attained fluency with single-digit multiplication, their fluency with more complex mathematical algorithms can develop more readily. Table 4.4 describes the steps for implementing fluency practice for algorithms.

Table 4.4: Steps for Implementing Fluency Practice for Algorithms

Implementation	Explanatory Notes for the Teacher
1. Determine which algorithm your students need to master to fluency. Select the skill, strategy, or process that is critically necessary for students' future success in school. Skills that are nice to know but will not generally be essential later do not need to be mastered to the fluency level.	Remember that fluency is a long-term goal in which you guide your students through earlier stages of practice and intentionally plan frequent structured practices and independent practices before moving to building fluency. Fluency is not about speed, per se, although students are always confronted with time limits during testing situations. Fluency suggests an ability to execute a skill, strategy, or process without a conscious effort. "Doing something without thinking" is one way of describing a process that is fluent.
2. Collect some type of baseline data for the skill.	Benchmark tests may provide the necessary information for more discrete skills. You may collect baseline data for more complex skills, strategies, or processes by using a rubric to determine how many students are at certain proficiency levels.
3. Determine if some students will need to acquire skills that were never learned or practiced to fluency at earlier grade levels.	This step in developing fluency for mathematical algorithms is a roadblock for far too many students. At the elementary or middle school level, a school-wide push to develop fluency for single-digit multiplication is a worthwhile endeavor.
4. Enlist students in setting goals and monitoring their own progress, and take time to reflect on what is working for them and what is holding them back.	Provide rubrics, anchor charts, and other supports to help students master the steps.
5. Intentionally plan practice sessions.	Students who are on the cusp of achieving fluency in a certain skill or process may need just a few more opportunities to practice. Shortchanging practice sessions to cover more material will, in the long run, interfere with your students' achieving fluency.
6. Carefully plan practice activities that expect increasing levels of proficiency in executing a specific grade-level standard.	Expert fluency comes only after teachers and learners have set the expectations for rigor continually higher. This requires your comprehensive knowledge of your students' precise achievement levels.

Implementation of Practice for Processes That Require Controlled Processing

Content that is procedural in nature requires that students be able to access critical declarative knowledge, process it adequately so as to understand it, and then move on to learning how to independently execute the process with fluency. To understand how controlled processing works, consider how you might develop fluency for the following secondary standard: *analyze how and why individuals, events, or ideas develop and interact over the course of a text* (CCR Anchor Standard 2, CCSS). The procedural skill embedded in this standard is *analyze*. Students are expected to execute one of the following:

- Analyze how a complex set of ideas develops and interacts over the course of a text.

- Analyze how a sequence of events develops and interacts over the course of a text.

- Analyze how various individuals develop and interact over the course of a text.

However, before they can execute any or all of these processes, they need to understand the meaning of the process involved in *analyzing.* They will need to understand what constitutes a sequence of events and how to track a sequence of events in a text. They will need to be able to identify ideas, events, and people as they read.

Before you can design practice activities to build fluency with a process such as this, you have some homework to do. Table 4.5 leads you through the steps to take before you will actually be ready to practice: identifying the critical content and processing it to the extent that students will understand what they are practicing and why. Identifying the critical content for students and then immediately fast-forwarding to practicing that content because there is so much to cover and you must move on may well result in failure for both you and your students.

Table 4.5: Sample Template for Practice to Build Fluency for Controlled Processing

PART 1: Teach the Conceptual Knowledge That Is Inherent in the Skill, Strategy, or Process	
Implementation	Explanatory Notes for the Teacher
1. Select the learning target for your fluency practice.	The learning target for this example is analyze how and why individuals, events, or ideas develop and interact over the course of a text.
2. Identify the critical content of the process you plan to teach.	What do students need to know and understand about the critical content to provide a foundation for acquiring the process?
3. Decide how you will facilitate the processing of this content.	Students will need to engage and process the first chunk of critical content.
PART 2: Do Before Your Practice Session	
1. Determine how you will chunk the process.	A process that requires controlled processing is by its nature more complicated.
2. Select the text in which students will read and respond in writing to what they have read.	Literacy (reading and writing) processes generally are executed in the course of reading a content text.
3. Develop supplementary materials, such as anchor charts or organizers, on which students can take notes.	A well-conceived anchor chart using student-friendly language can help students keep track of the steps in a process.
PART 3: Practice the Skill, Strategy, or Process	
1. Identify the step or part of the process you want students to practice.	Students are more likely to have success developing fluency with a process if you begin with just a "baby step" so they can feel successful.

2. Model and demonstrate the process.	Once students have a basic understanding of the first step of the process, teacher can move to the next step: showing them how to execute that chunk. For example, if teacher's first chunk of the process is to show students how to analyze a sequence of events, he has already defined analyzing for students, and they have processed the meaning of the word by looking at examples and nonexamples he has shown them. They have also had opportunities to talk with a partner. Now it is time to demonstrate how he would analyze a sequence of events using a short sample text. Teacher first thinks-aloud while orally reading the text he will analyze.
3. Provide once or twice a week opportunities to practice analyzing a sequence of events in a short sample text and writing a brief response.	Teacher provides students with an organizer in which to record their analysis of how the author shows how the events develop and interact and why.
4. As students develop fluency in the process of analyzing how an author shows how events in a text develop and interact and why, move on to analyzing ideas and individuals.	Developing fluency in the execution of a multi-step process requires practice. Your challenge is to provide frequent opportunities to practice this process in a variety of texts.

Common Mistakes

The most common mistakes teachers make when first implementing fluency practice include the following:

- The teacher fails to identify the critical declarative knowledge that is foundational to developing fluency.

- The teacher emphasizes speed before students are comfortable with the discrete skills or steps.

- The teacher expects students to practice procedural knowledge that is too challenging.

- The teacher fails to prioritize which types of procedural knowledge are worthy of fluency practice.

- The teacher fails to provide enough opportunities for fluency practice in the classroom.

- The teacher fails to monitor students' development of fluency.

Examples and Nonexamples of Fluency Practice

Following are examples and nonexamples of fluency practice in elementary and secondary classrooms. As you read, reflect on the ways that the example teachers have effectively implemented the technique and pay close attention to the mistakes the nonexample teachers have made.

Elementary Example of Fluency Practice for Controlled Processing

The learning target for this elementary example is *retell stories, including key details, and demonstrate understanding of their central message or lesson* (CCSS.ELA-Literacy.RL.1.2). This learning target is an example of a literacy process that requires controlled processing.

A first-grade teacher is working with her students to develop fluency in their retelling of stories. This example is divided into two sections: 1) a sample template that will enable you to gain a complete perspective of the lesson steps and 2) a classroom scenario describing the specific aspect of fluency practice for a skill requiring controlled processing.

Sample Lesson Template for Fluency Practice of a Process Requiring Controlled Processing: First-Grade Literacy

Table 4.5 is a lesson template showing the steps for fluency practice of a process requiring controlled processing. Part 1 enumerates the steps for teaching the concepts and vocabulary needed as the foundation for building fluency. Part 2 describes the actual practice session.

Table 4.5: Sample Lesson Template for Fluency Practice: First-Grade Literacy

PART 1: Teach the Conceptual Knowledge That Is the Foundation for the Skill, Strategy, or Process	
Implementation	Explanatory Notes for the Teacher
1. Select the learning target for which you will implement close monitoring.	The learning target is *retell stories, including key details, and demonstrate understanding of their central message or lesson* (CCSS.ELA-Literacy.RL.1.2).
2. Identify the critical content that you will initially teach your students prior to the practice session.	Students will need to be able to understand the vocabulary and concepts that are inherent in executing the process in the learning target: what constitutes a detail and how to tell the difference between a key detail and a trivial detail; how to figure out if the story has a central message or lesson (i.e., a moral).
3. Identify the ways in which students will process the critical content they need to understand as a foundation to practicing the skill.	Students will process the critical content in chunks. On some occasions they will retell a story that has been read aloud. On other occasions they will find details in a story they are reading in their guided reading group. This kind of processing may take several weeks.
PART 2: Practice the Skill, Strategy, or Process	
1. Determine the task you want students to practice during their practice session.	Students have been practicing various aspects of the learning target, but today is the first time they will practice the process as a whole.
2. Model the task.	Teacher models the process for students, thinking aloud about how she plans to include all three aspects of the retelling of her story. She is modeling in text that students have previously read so as not to overload their working memories with a brand-new story while they are acquiring the process.
3. Read aloud a familiar story to students.	Not only is teacher modeling from a familiar text, but also the story she reads aloud to them is one that has been previously read.
4. Ask students to practice the process with their partners while you observe, making sure all students in the group are on track.	Teacher provides the students with an anchor chart to help them remember the steps in the process.

(continued on next page)

Table 4.5: Sample Lesson Template for Fluency Practice: First-Grade Literacy *(continued)*

PART 2: Practice the Skill, Strategy, or Process *(continued)*	
5. Teacher coaches, prompts, and praises students as appropriate.	Students will practice this process multiple times in the coming weeks, gaining fluency with the process.
6. Students debrief their practice session.	Students relate the ways they remember the steps in the process and how they pay attention while they are reading the text or listening to the teacher read aloud.

Classroom Scenario Implementing Fluency Practice: First-Grade Literacy

Until this point of the practice session in the scenario, the teacher has focused instruction on the discrete skills or steps that her students must master, such as understanding how story events are typically organized into a beginning, a middle, and an end; picking out key details in a story; and identifying the central message, or moral, of the story. Her students are able to successfully execute each of the discrete skills fluently, but she wants them to develop a level of fluency that will transfer to their independent reading of text as well as their listening comprehension when stories are read aloud in class. She realizes that the mastery of this standard using grade-level text is important for her students' future success in school and beyond, and she is committed to developing this process to grade-level-appropriate fluency.

She introduces her retelling fluency goal to her students as follows:

> Boys and girls, during the past few weeks we have learned how to retell a story. You have learned that a retelling of a story has to have three things: 1) it has to describe the beginning, the middle, and the end of the story; 2) it has to tell the key details; and 3) it has to infer the message, or moral, of the story. Our learning target for the next few weeks is to develop fluency in retelling stories. Fluency means that you can retell the story, including these three things, easily and quickly. To

develop fluency, we need to practice retelling stories two times every day at school and one time at home every night. In the beginning, we're going to retell familiar stories. But soon, we'll be retelling every story we read together during reading class, stories you read at your stations, stories the librarian or I read aloud to you, and the stories your family or caregiver read to you after school.

The implementation of this type of fluency practice is new to the teacher. She has enlisted the support of parents or caregivers and provided them with a template and suggestions for practicing the retelling of short read-alouds that go home in special book bags.

The teacher collects baseline data from each student using a retelling rubric she developed. She shares the fluency data with each student, and then the class as a whole sets some goals for increasing their fluency in retelling stories. She is able to see where students need mini-lessons on one or more aspects of the retelling process and also track how students are becoming more fluent in their abilities to retell a story that includes each of the discrete skills that she has taught. The success of fluency practice focused on the story retelling standard encourages her to design fluency practice for other standards that has given her students difficulty during both formative and summative assessments.

Elementary Nonexample of Fluency Practice

The nonexample teacher is focused on the same learning target: *retell stories, including key details, and demonstrate understanding of their central message or lesson* (CCSS.ELA-Literacy.RL.1.2). Similarly to the example teacher, the first-grade nonexample teacher has been discouraged by her students' ability to gain fluency in retelling stories. She would like to devote class time to fluency practice but feels pressured to cover all of the stories in the reader before the end of the school year. She decides that she will enlist parents' help by sending home a set of instructions and a story bag. However, she omits the two most important aspects of the fluency equation—enlisting her students in setting fluency goals individually and as a class and collecting weekly data to see how students' retelling fluency is improving.

Secondary Example of Fluency Practice for Automaticity and Accuracy

The learning target for the secondary fluency practice example is *interpret and compute quotients of fractions, and solve word problems involving division of fractions by fractions* (CCSS.Math.Content.6.NS.A.1). This example demonstrates how a middle school teacher is building fluency for a mathematical algorithm: dividing fractions. The example is divided into two sections: 1) a sample template that will make it easier for you to place the fluency building practice in the context of earlier instruction and 2) a classroom scenario describing the specific aspect of the instruction that is devoted to practice.

Sample Lesson Template for Fluency Practice: Sixth-Grade Math

Table 4.6 is a sample lesson template illustrating fluency-building practice with an algorithm. Part 1 describes the conceptual knowledge students need to acquire before they can engage in productive fluency-building practice. Part 2 describes the steps the teacher must complete before the practice sessions, while Part 3 describes the flow of the practice.

Table 4.6: Sample Lesson Template for Fluency Practice: Sixth-Grade Math

PART 1: Teach the Conceptual Knowledge That Is Inherent in the Skill, Strategy, or Process	
Implementation	Explanatory Notes for the Teacher
1. Select the learning target for which you will implement fluency building.	The learning target is *interpret and compute quotients of fractions, and solve word problems involving division of fractions by fractions* (CCSS.Math.Content.6.NS.A.1).
2. Identify the critical content that you will initially teach your students prior to developing fluency.	Students will need extensive opportunities to develop the conceptual framework that underlies the division of fractions by fractions to include opportunities to connect physical models to symbolic representations. Students will need a conceptual understanding of whether a division problem is a quotitive (measurement) division problem or a partitive (sharing) division problem.

3. Identify the ways in which students will process the critical content they need to understand as a foundation to practicing the skill.	Students need multiple opportunities to use worked examples of word problems illustrating both types of problems.
4. Provide various types of practice to build the discrete skills that are a part of this algorithm to include building fluency with single-digit multiplication.	Teacher practices solving a mix of both types of word problems while also building fluency with single-digit multiplication.
PART 2: Do Before Your Practice Session	
1. Develop an anchor chart for division of fractions if needed.	Anchor charts can actually impede fluency if students come to depend on them for every step of a skill.
2. Determine how frequently the practice sessions will occur.	The practice sessions occur during a five-minute math warm-up at the beginning of each class.
3. Develop practice sets of problems.	Teacher determines how many problems will be in each set and how much time students will have to complete the problems.
4. Develop a student progress chart.	Figure 4.4 is an example of a student progress chart.
PART 3: Practice the Skill, Strategy, or Process	
1. Determine the task you want students to practice during their fluency-building practice sessions.	Accurately and automatically solve computational and word problems containing division of fractions.
2. Place pages with the problem sets down on students' desks.	Students write the number of problems they want to solve during the practice session.
3. Teacher asks students to practice while she observes, making sure all students in the group are practicing correctly.	Teacher encourages students to construct drawings or imagine physical representations of the word problems they solve.
4. Teacher provides answers to the problems while students grade their own papers.	The problems students find on these practice tests are not as challenging as those the teacher will use during upcoming varied practice sessions as in Instructional Technique 5.
5. Students enter their results on a progress-measuring chart.	Figure 4.4 contains a sample of a student progress chart.

Classroom Scenario Implementing Fluency Practice:
Sixth-Grade Math

The example sixth-grade teacher provides his students with many opportunities to practice dividing fractions. Although he assigns more complex and challenging problems to be solved for homework, as is in Instructional Technique 5, varied practice, the purpose of fluency practice is to build endurance, stamina, and a measure of speed. He has taught this skill during an earlier unit, but it continues to be one that students practice at least once or twice a week using a variety of problems, including word problems, to build fluency. During the unit on the division of fractions by fractions, the teacher teaches students the steps for dividing fractions and makes sure they develop the math concepts and vocabulary they need for success in advance. At the beginning of class each day, students engage in a five-minute math warm-up to practice solving problems that require the use of skills and strategies taught in previous units. Developing fluency with this process is crucial to future success in higher-level mathematics classes.

The teacher places papers face down on student desks. Students begin by writing their goal for the number of problems they want to solve during the warm-up. This number is based on the highest number achieved during previous practice sessions. As soon as the timer starts, students work alone to solve as many problems as possible. The teacher then posts answers and students self-check problems. Students chart their own progress. Figure 4.4 is an example of the chart the students use. The teacher asks students to reflect briefly on their practice session. One student shares: *"When I come to a problem that is really challenging, it helps me to think about similar problems I have solved. The problem about the one-half of the pizza being divided into sixths is similar to the cookie problem we did in class. In the cookie problem, I drew a picture of one-third of the cookies being divided into fourths. So I drew a picture of half of a pizza and then thought about how many sixths are in the half. It really helps me to solve problems quickly when I make connections to former problems. That's why I can solve more problems in five minutes that I used to be able to do."*

Figure 4.4: Example of Student Progress Chart

Progress Measurement	Practice Sessions				
	1	2	3	4	5
Number of Problems I Attempted to Solve					
Number of Problems I Solved Correctly					

Adapted from Marzano (2007).

Secondary Nonexample of Fluency Practice

The nonexample teacher is focused on the same learning target: *interpret and compute quotients of fractions, and solve word problems involving division of fractions by fractions* (CCSS.Math.Content.6.NS.A.1). She expects her students to engage in fluency practice at home each night but has not devised an accountability method that includes both parents and students. The teacher has not provided an anchor chart for students to take home nor do they have access to a video of their teacher (or another math teacher) modeling the algorithm. Students turn in homework at the beginning of class; but the teacher does not take the time to go over their work. Students do not track their progress or reflect on how they are gaining speed in solving the problems. Many students either do not turn in homework or engage in sharing work with students who did not understand or simply did not do the homework.

Determining If Students Have Developed Fluency With a Skill, Strategy, or Process

You will know that your students have developed fluency with a skill, strategy, or process only by monitoring their progress. Here are several ways to determine if students are making progress toward the desired result:

- As students respond to practice problems, exercises, and constructed responses using mini response boards, scan their work and clarify as needed to ensure continued success with similar practice tasks.

- Have students practice a skill, strategy, or process, and ask them to write a sentence about how their practice increased their fluency.

- Ask students to describe how practice activities have influenced or deepened their understanding.

- Review student responses for automaticity, accuracy, fluency, and controlled processing.

Use the student proficiency scale in Table 4.7 to determine how well your students are progressing toward the desired result as you provide various types of fluency practice for them.

Table 4.7: Student Proficiency Scale for Practicing Skills, Strategies, and Processes Using Fluency Practice

Emerging	Fundamental	Desired Result
Students mechanically use the steps in the skill, strategy, or process.	Students use the steps in the skill, strategy, or process easily or smoothly.	Students use the steps in the skill, strategy, or process with automatic or controlled processing.
Students are aware they are practicing for fluency.	Students are aware they are increasing their fluency.	Students can explain how their thinking has changed over time to increase fluency in the skill, strategy, or process.
Students set appropriate goals for fluency practice.	Students set appropriate goals for fluency practice and track their growth in accuracy or automaticity.	Students set appropriate goals for fluency practice and track their growth in accuracy and automaticity over time.
Students are confident they are able to attempt the skill, strategy, or process.	Students are confident in some components of the skill, strategy, or process.	Students are confident in their ability to use the skill, strategy, or process.

Scaffold and Extend Instruction to Meet Students' Needs

You will undoubtedly encounter the challenge of working with students who need extra support as they work to develop fluency in a skill or process. Conversely, there will be students who are already fluent in your grade-level standards and need to have their learning opportunities extended.

Scaffolding

- Break skills or processes into smaller chunks that students can practice separately before putting them together in a fluent skill, strategy, or process.

- Help students create a checklist or a series of small goals to help them experience success while continuing to improve fluency.

- Select online videos that demonstrate a skill, strategy, or process along with clear verbal explanations and graphics. Encourage students to work along with the video, stopping and starting it to practice a particularly challenging step.

Extending

- Ask students to describe each step of the skill, strategy, or process and how it has led them to their current level of fluency.

- Ask students to describe techniques that helped them make large increases in their automatic or controlled processing.

- Ask students to develop tutorials or videos to share their techniques with other students.

Instructional Technique 5

VARIED PRACTICE

Varied practice consists of using newly acquired procedural knowledge in a variety of different situations. During prior practice experiences, tasks and problems have likely been more predictable for students, and until now you have been guiding and monitoring that practice or building fluency. However, at some point, and only you can determine whether and when your students reach that plateau, more of the same type of practice becomes a waste of time. Students can write answers on practice sheets while their minds are elsewhere. The practice is not demanding enough to engage students' attention, and they do not have opportunities to refine and shape their procedural knowledge. Varied practice is independent. During varied practice, students are expected to meet the challenge of encountering a task or problem in a completely different format or context than they did during their previous practice sessions, and to do it without your close supervision or even direct assistance.

You may also be challenged as you seek to design opportunities for varied practice. Typical textbooks and curriculum guides often focus on practice exercises that are the same or very similar to the taught lesson. However, to achieve the rigor that is required as students tackle more challenging standards, varied practice must meld students' conceptual understanding, fluency in the execution of procedural skills, and the ability to apply that declarative and procedural knowledge in new and varied ways.

A simple example illustrates the essence of varied practice. When students have learned how to solve a mathematical problem in one way, the typical practice exercise consists of problems that can all be solved by using the taught method. The content is mathematics, and the learning target is patterning. If students have practiced patterning as ABABAB, then they will not know what to do when they encounter XOXOXO. In varied practice, the teacher will present a variety of object patterns so students can apply the skill of recognizing two object patterns to any two objects. Varied practice gives students opportunities as well as challenges to apply a specific skill or strategy to a unique or more complex task. Undoubtedly many, if not most, students will experience some frustration when they encounter a different task or problem from the ones they have practiced, but only when students can meet the challenge of varied practice will they achieve rigor.

How to Effectively Implement Varied Practice

The effective implementation of varied practice requires the creation of challenging tasks and problems in which students can practice critical content and then ensure that they experience success in meeting and overcoming these challenges. Implementing varied practice not only requires that your students notch up the rigor of their practice activities but also requires that you have a deep understanding of your content to enable you to design the tasks. Part 1 of Table 5.1 illustrates the steps that must precede varied practice, while the actual practice sessions are in Part 2.

Table 5.1: A Sample Lesson Template for Effectively Implementing Varied Practice

PART 1: Teach the Conceptual Knowledge That Is Essential to the Skill, Strategy, or Process	
Implementation	Explanatory Notes for the Teacher
1. Identify the learning target you want your students to fully master in a rigorous way.	As soon as you identify the learning target, begin to design and collect exemplars of varied practice that you will expect your students to apply and extend their previous understandings of this target.
2. Teach and then ensure that students process the critical concepts and ideas that form the foundation of the critical content.	Avoid the temptation to shortcut your students' acquisition of conceptual knowledge in an effort to fast-forward to the targeted skill or process.
3. Design practice that you closely monitor to ensure students are practicing the skill, strategy, or process accurately.	So students will get off to a solid start in the skill, strategy, or process, model and think aloud for them or provide worked examples to which they can self-regulate and self-question as they practice the skill, strategy, or process.
4. Once you have launched students, provide frequent structured practice to solidify the skill, strategy, or process.	Instructional Technique 3 provides suggestions for how to use frequent structured practice.
5. Following the lead of your students' progress and mastery, begin to build fluency with the skill, strategy, or process.	Instructional Technique 4 provides suggestions for how to build fluency.

6. As you engage in fluency practice, begin to assess your students' readiness for varied practice. The list in the adjoining column is intended to be illustrative since many of the states are similar in nature. However, the essence of readiness for varied practice is conceptual understanding and a growing fluency in executing the procedural knowledge.	Students are ready to transition to practice activities that require more independence and self-management techniques when they can successfully execute one or more of the following aspects of the critical content: ● paraphrase or summarize the critical or essential elements of the skill, strategy, or process ● describe how to or why use the skill, strategy, or process ● describe the key parts of a skill, strategy, or process ● describe the relationship between the parts or steps in the skill, strategy, or process ● explain when the skill, strategy, or process should be used ● execute the components of the skill, strategy, or process
PART 2: Practice the Skill or Process in Varied Ways	
1. Select the skills, strategies, or processes you will assign to students.	The most frequent type of varied practice for mathematics involves designing word problems that require unique applications of the skill, strategy, or process. The most frequent type of varied practice for literacy skills is cross-disciplinary. Once a skill or process has been acquired and fluency is developing, varied practice includes reading text from social studies, science, or ELA and executing a process with a particular text from a specific discipline.
2. Determine how students will practice: on their own or in some type of cooperative group. While some students are engaged in independent varied practice, you will have short periods of time in which you can provide other types of practice for students who are not ready for varied practice.	There are many ways to organize students into small groups or partner teams to engage in varied practice. You can easily meet the challenges of this type of practice if students can work together toward a goal.
3. Determine how you will monitor students' progress.	If you are not working with other groups of students, walk around and scan what students are doing or you could collect work products from each set of partners.

Common Mistakes

Following are some of the common mistakes the teacher can easily make as you initially implement varied practice:

- The teacher fails to formatively assess students to determine their readiness for varied practice.

- The teacher fails to match the rigor of the practice activity to the cognitive complexity of the learning target or standard he is addressing.

- The teacher fails to design practice that goes deeper into the content.

- The teacher fails to match the application of the procedural knowledge to students' current skill levels.

- The teacher fails to push students into more than one varied practice session before moving on to another learning target.

Examples and Nonexamples Using Varied Practice

The effective use of varied practice in the classroom requires knowing when students are ready to move beyond close monitoring and frequent structured practice to more complex and rigorous varied practice activities. Following are examples and nonexamples of varied practice from elementary and secondary classrooms.

Elementary Example of Varied Practice

This example demonstrates how an elementary teacher uses varied practice with her third-grade students. The example is divided into two parts: 1) a completed planning template that will enable you to understand the flow of the lesson and 2) a classroom scenario describing the lesson represented in the template.

Sample Planning Template for Implementing Varied Practice: Third-Grade Math

Table 5.1 contains a planning template illustrating varied practice in a third-grade math class.

Figure 5.1 Sample Template for Implementing Varied Practice: Third-Grade Math

Implementation	Explanatory Notes for the Teacher
1. Identify the learning target that requires varied practice opportunities.	The learning target for this example is *use multiplication and division within 100 to solve word problems in situations involving equal groups, arrays, and measurement quantities, e.g., by using drawings and equations with a symbol for the unknown number to represent the problem* (3.OA.A.3.CCSS Mathematics).
2. Describe the varied practice task you will assign to students.	Solve word problems with problems multiplying three or more numbers. For example, students at Brad's school sold magazine subscriptions to earn money for a field trip. Ten students sold 6 subscriptions and collected $5 per subscription. How much money did the students earn? Write an equation with a symbol for the unknown number.
3. Identify the way you plan to group students.	Students will work with their assigned partners on the task.
4. Determine how you will monitor students' progress.	During this first experience with varied practice, teacher spends time walking around the room and listening to students' conversations. She will be available for questions, but will confine her answers to prompting and encouraging students to work through their challenges.
5. Make notes of students' progress in varied practice.	As students become accustomed to the challenges of varied practice and develop endurance and confidence about their abilities to solve difficult problems, you can gradually notch up the difficulty level of practice activities.
6. Debrief with students regarding their success/frustrations and also what new insights they gained into applying previous learning to the new task.	Identify any aspects of the skill in which teacher needs to reteach some critical conceptual knowledge to increase students' success with varied practice.

Classroom Scenario for Implementing Varied Practice: Third-Grade Math

The example teacher has been working with her students over several weeks on learning targets related to operations and algebraic thinking. The students have developed fluency with single-digit multiplication and division problems and are able to represent and solve problems involving multiplication and division. She believes they are ready to solve a mix of word problems involving 1) multiplying three or more numbers, 2) missing factors, and 3) division word problems. Students are working with partners on a set of six problems. Here is how she introduces the practice session:

> Class, today you are going to work on six challenging math problems. The good news is that you get to work with a partner. You have learned all of the math skills that you need to solve these problems. The challenge is that they are what we call **real-world problems**. Some teachers call them **word problems.** You will need to apply all of the lessons you have learned in math class during the past few weeks. If you get stuck, just imagine that you and your partner are on a desert island and to get off the island, you have to come up with the right answers to these problems.

The teacher goes over the partner assignments and passes out the varied practice sheet. While students are working, she walks around the room, listening in on conversations. She reminds students to label their answers and check their work. Her students are generally doing quite well on the practice set and the teacher is already figuring out the varied practice assignment she plans to use at the beginning of her class the next day.

Elementary Nonexample of Varied Practice

The elementary nonexample teacher has designed a practice sheet that is somewhat similar to the example teacher's varied practice assignment. However, he chooses a different approach for his students' first attempt. Rather than having students work in pairs, he decides to make this an independent homework assignment. Of course, the teacher would be unavailable to encourage and prompt students through some early frustration, and his email box will be filled with messages from parents who are upset that students were sent home to practice such difficult problems.

Secondary Example of Varied Practice

This secondary example demonstrates how a grades 5–8 middle school math teacher uses varied practice with his fifth-grade students. The example is divided into two parts: 1) a completed planning template that will enable you to understand the flow of the lesson and 2) a classroom scenario describing the lesson represented in the template.

Sample Template for Implementing Varied Practice:
Fifth-Grade Math

Table 5.2: Sample Template for Implementing Varied Practice:
Fifth-Grade Math

Implementation	Explanatory Notes for the Teacher
1. Identify the learning target that requires varied practice opportunities.	The specific learning target in this example is *apply and extend previous understandings of multiplication and division.*
2. Explain the varied practice activity. The standards in Column 2 provide the content for the varied practice. The learning target is at a more cognitively complex level and requires students to apply and extend this content.	Students will *find the area of a rectangle with fractional side lengths by tiling it with unit squares of the appropriate unit fraction side lengths, and show that the area is the same as would be found by multiplying the side lengths to find areas of rectangles and represent fraction products as rectangular areas* (CCSS.Math.Content.5.NF.B.4b). or Students will also *solve real-world problems involving division of unit fraction by non-zero whole numbers and division of whole numbers by unit fractions by using visual fraction models and equations to represent the problem* (CCSS.Math.Content.5.NF.B7c).
3. Identify the way you plan to group students.	Students will be working with partners.
4. Determine how you will monitor students' progress.	Teacher walks around listening in and scanning students' practice sheets.

(continued on next page)

Table 5.2: Sample Template for Implementing Varied Practice: Fifth-Grade Math *(continued)*

Implementation	Explanatory Notes for the Teacher
5. Make notes of students' progress in varied practice.	The teacher records her notes on her clipboard or in her grade book.
6. Make notes on the success and challenges of the varied practice.	Teacher develops a list of questions to ask students.
7. Debrief with students regarding their success and frustrations and also what new insights they gained into applying previous learning to the new task.	Teacher determines whether students need reteaching of any key concepts.

Classroom Scenario for Implementing Varied Practice: Fifth-Grade Math

The secondary example for implementing varied practice takes place in a middle school math class. The varied practice is designed to apply and extend previous understandings of multiplication and division. The teacher has spent more class time working on mathematical concepts and attempting to guide his students to understandings of mathematics as more that memorizing a list of steps to solve a problem. Most students have developed fluency with single-digit multiplication and it is time for more rigorous application of the critical content. He is hoping that the combination of solid concepts and procedural fluency will help his students solve the challenging problems he has put together for their first varied practice session. Here is how he introduces the practice session to his students:

> Good morning, class. Today is kind of an experiment for me. *His class sits up a little straighter in their seats.* You probably didn't realize, but I've taught this unit quite a bit differently this year than I have in the past, and today I'm going to find out whether that was a good idea. The results that you give me on this set of practice problems is going to provide evidence for my new method or it's going to make me question my decision.

The good news is that you are the smartest class that I have ever had. You understand more about mathematical concepts and have more speed when you're working problems than any class I've ever had. The question is, will you be able to apply this knowledge to some challenging problems? You won't have to work on your own. You'll work with a partner. I'm not going to be there to look over your shoulder as I have done during some other practice sessions. I want to see how independent you can be and how well you can handle something that's a bit more difficult. These problems will take perseverance.

After that introduction, the teacher puts the partners together, passes out the practice sheets and reminds students not to give up when the problem does not solve itself in the first three seconds. The teacher is impressed with the way his students begin working and pleased as he walks around checking what is going on with the various pairs of students. He is beginning to believe that his experiment is a success. He can hardly wait to share it with the math department team.

Secondary Nonexample of Varied Practice

The nonexample teacher has taken a different approach to the learning target than her counterpart across the hall. She has focused solely on developing automaticity with single-digit multiplication and division and practicing the algorithms using a more rigid step-by-step fashion. She felt too rushed to spend time on building conceptual understandings but does not really think that her students have missed much. Just for fun, she picks up the varied practice test that her colleague is giving to his students. The problems look a bit difficult, but she decides to give it to her students. They struggle with the test, and ultimately more than three-quarters of her class is unable to solve even half of the problems.

Determining If Students Are Proficient in Using Varied Practice

You will know if your students have developed the desired level of proficiency through the varied practice sessions you have provided for them only if you are constantly monitoring their progress. Use the following suggestions, and then begin to develop your own menu of ways to monitor this technique:

- Walk around the room and listen to students as they discuss the skill, strategy, or process with partners to ensure they are overcoming challenges and obstacles.

- Have students complete exit tickets summarizing the insights they have developed from their varied practice sessions.

- Use various types of technology on which students can write or record their answers that you can then download to use as a formative assessment of the practice session.

- Ask students to monitor their own practice with the skill, strategy, or process and identify their strengths and weaknesses. Use this information to monitor their progress.

Use the student proficiency scale in Table 5.3 to determine how well your students are progressing toward the desired result of this technique.

Table 5.3: Student Proficiency Scale for Practicing Skills, Strategies, and Processes Using Varied Practice

Emerging	Fundamental	Desired Result
Students attempt to overcome challenges and obstacles.	Students overcome challenges and obstacles.	Students easily overcome challenges and obstacles.
Students can use newly acquired procedural knowledge in situations that the teacher taught.	Students use newly acquired procedural knowledge in a variety of different situations.	Students fluently use newly acquired procedural knowledge in a variety of different situations.
Students can identify when they should use the skill, strategy, or process.	Students can explain why they should use the skill, strategy, or process.	Students can describe specific situations when they should use the skill, strategy, or process.

Scaffold and Extend Instruction to Meet Students' Needs

Varied practice may prove to be a struggle for some of your students, while others will eagerly embrace the complexity and challenge. Meeting the needs of these two diverse groups of students requires that you adapt your instruction. Here are some ways for developing scaffolding and extending to meet students' needs.

Scaffolding

- Spend more time with hands-on manipulatives for varied practice in mathematics.

- Provide students with anchor charts to help them navigate more difficult literacy processes.

- Divide tasks into more manageable chunks to avoid overloading students' working memories.

- Give fewer problems for varied practice.

- Give easier reading texts in which to execute reading and writing processes.

Extending

- Increase the number of problems or length of the text so that students can develop stamina in their use of procedural knowledge.

- Provide new situations in which the procedural knowledge is required. Change the context so that students understand that this knowledge is not isolated to one subject area or type of text. Ask students to analyze the situation and explain how the procedural knowledge is used.

- Once students are comfortable with the fundamentals of the skill or strategy, add a new layer to the procedural knowledge. For example, show the reverse of using a math operation. If students can subtract with borrowing, they should understand place value. Have students check their answer by using addition.

- Practice two or more skills required to successfully execute a process. When learning a process, such as editing, they will need to learn the rules of capitalization and punctuation and practice these rules separately during guided practice. When students comprehend the rules (declarative knowledge) and have been successful at editing for each convention separately, provide students with tasks that incorporate both skills. Students will need rubrics or checklists to use to self-monitor. At the end of each practice session, ask students to share any new awareness they have achieved regarding the strategy.

- As students become fluent thinkers using the target procedural knowledge, have them create their own problems and show how to use the strategy. Ask them to change the situation or variables without changing the operations. Give students index cards to write a new problem on the front and work the problem on the back. Collect the cards and select some of the problems for the class to use for review.

- Have students use applications, such as Educreations (available at www.educreations.com), to create lessons that other students can use as tutorials. For English language arts, have students create podcasts or vodcasts in which they use the procedural knowledge in creative ways.

Instructional Technique 6

PRACTICE BEFORE TESTS

Whether students are taking a unit test or a standardized test, they will benefit from carefully planned practice sessions. In anticipation of practicing for summative tests, collect formative data to identify which learning targets need the most intensive practice. Develop a set of priorities for which skills, strategies, and processes need the most attention. A productive practice schedule allots time for meaningful practice matched to each student's current level of mastery. Some students need additional practice to deepen their understandings of the declarative knowledge necessary to successfully execute the skills, strategies, and processes, while others many need practice to help overcome test anxiety. With so much depending on how well your students perform, it is critical to establish an action plan that maximizes practice time and provides just the right practice for each student.

How to Effectively Implement Practice Before Testing

There are two ways to approach practice sessions prior to testing: 1) schedule ongoing practice of critical content throughout the school year or 2) schedule practice of critical content a short time (about one month) before taking the test.

Scheduling Ongoing Practice of Critical Content Throughout the School Year

Any type of performance requires rehearsals. The band, orchestra, sports teams, and speech and debate teams all practice intensely throughout the school year for end-of-season or end-of year performances. These teams do not wait until a month before their big performance. They begin practicing when school starts in the fall and continue to rehearse regularly, in some cases every day. If you and your colleagues know you will feel overwhelmed with test preparation in the spring , plan ahead by rehearsing critical content all year long.

Table 6.1 enumerates the steps of a plan for organizing your classroom—or even your campus—to practice for upcoming summative tests. Follow the steps at the beginning of the school year to identify where your students need to preemptively practice during the academic year *or* use the plan to schedule short-term practice sessions for students who need a final push to get ready for a test.

Table 6.1: Sample Plan for Effectively Organizing Practice Before a Test

Implementation	Explanatory Notes for the Teacher
1. Review the grade level or subject matter standards that will be tested.	Identify those standards that are most difficult to master. You may need to allocate more practice time for standards that are the most critical for college and career readiness.
2. Use student data to create practice groups focused on specific standards.	Consider what type of practice is needed—frequent structured, varied, or fluency. Decide how you will group students. Homogeneous groups allow for differentiation or personalized learning. Heterogeneous cooperative groups enable more proficient students to deepen their understanding while supporting less proficient students.
3. Have students identify and commit to personal learning goals.	Have learners reflect on their levels of mastery and what they might do to increase their proficiency levels.
4. Create a calendar that outlines a practice schedule to ensure that students have adequate time to review and practice skills, strategies, and processes before they are tested.	You might provide a fixed number of test practice minutes each day or week. Consider specifying a day each week or throughout a unit to study to practice previously mastered skill, strategies, or processes. This type of practice can build fluency.
5. Identify practice activities matched to the learning goals.	Practice should include both in-class activities and homework assignments. Provide students with a variety of resources during practice sessions. Many students need varied practice that requires using knowledge in a variety of situations over time to fluently recall and apply the knowledge to testing situations.
6. Institute a method for students to track their progress during practice.	When students can see their upward trends in fluency, their motivation to persevere will increase.

Common Mistakes

Be aware of the following common mistakes that can easily derail the teacher's efforts to structure practice sessions before students face a high-stakes standardized test:

- The teacher is overly focused on "the test" rather than developing fluency for critical skills, strategies, and processes.

- The teacher overwhelms students by scheduling too many intensive practice sessions for too many skills, strategies, or processes.

- The teacher fails to identify and communicate the standards or learning targets to students.

- The teacher gives students too many test-taking strategies rather than providing varied practice opportunities that deepen critical content.

- The teacher fails to provide students with cognitively complex learning opportunities for each targeted standard.

- The teacher fails to engage students in setting goals for the test-taking experience.

Examples and Nonexamples of Practice Before Tests

Following are two examples (one elementary and one secondary) and their corresponding nonexamples of using practice before a testing situation. Compare the examples to your own experiences and consider the common mistakes. Note how example teachers strategically avoid them and nonexample teachers miss opportunities to structure productive practice.

Elementary Example of Short-Term Practice Before Tests

The example teacher is preparing her fifth-grade students for the summative mathematics assessment. Figure 6.1 displays the standards she has targeted for intensive practice during the twenty class days before the test.

Figure 6.1: Fifth-Grade Math Standards to Practice Before Test

• Add and subtract fractions with unlike denominators (including mixed numbers) by replacing given fractions with equivalent fractions in such a way as to produce an equivalent sum or difference of fractions with like denominators (CCSS.Math.Content.5.NFA.1).
• Solve word problems involving addition and subtraction of fractions referring to the same whole, including cases of unlike denominators (CCSS.Math.Content.5.NF.A.2).
• Use parentheses, brackets, or braces in numerical expressions and evaluation expression with these symbols (CCSS.Math.Content.5.OA.A.1).
• Write simple expressions that record calculations with number and interpret numerical expressions without evaluating them (CCSS.Math.Content.5.OA.A.2).

To begin, the teacher confers with each student and reviews strengths and areas for growth. Students set goals and identify math stations they will go to during independent practice time. The teacher provides guided practice for standards in areas that students are below 60 percent on all benchmark assessments.

Each day during the countdown to the test, students begin with a ten-minute math review that they complete with partners. The teacher gives students one problem and one pencil. They must discuss the problem and share the pencil to create a visual using the problem-solving process. Problems are aligned with the level of rigor specified in each standard, so there is an element of challenge for students.

A five-minute focus lesson follows the practice. The content of the lesson is determined by the two to four standards in which most students have scored below the mastery level in previous years and are still struggling in the current school year. The teacher models her thinking and refers to the anchor chart created earlier in the year that contains the declarative knowledge needed to successfully perform the procedural knowledge. She engages students by asking tiered questions that require students to make suggestions for solving the problem and provide reasoning to support the suggestions.

After the focus lesson, students work at math stations or in a small group with the teacher. One of the goals is for students to build math problem-solving stamina, so practice time is at least thirty to forty-five minutes. Students demonstrate accountability for their practice by completing an activity exit ticket before moving on to another practice activity or station. When time is called, the class gathers and debriefs their practice. Students must be able to elaborate on how this practice helps them become better problem solvers. They explain any challenges they faced and also what strategies they used to overcome those challenges.

During each of the four Fridays in the month prior to the test, students take a twenty-minute assessment. The teacher tracks their progress on a chart showing the number of problems attempted and the number of problems accurately solved. Students set a goal for the next assessment and write a reflection of what they need to do to improve. The teacher reviews the reflections the students have written about where they need to improve and sends the reflections home for parents to review and sign.

Elementary Nonexample of Short-Term Practice Before Tests

The nonexample class will also be taking the state math assessment in about a month. The teacher has prepared lesson plans that include test practice from a math workbook purchased specifically to help students prepare for the test. Each day, students are given three pages in the workbook to complete. The students complete the first page with the teacher, and he models how to solve the problems as students follow along. Students complete the second page with a partner and take the third page home for homework. The teacher wants parents to be aware of the difficult problems students will face on the real test. The math workbook addresses all math standards, so all standards are practiced equally regardless of whether practice is needed.

The teacher has left the test practice design up to the publisher. Without examining student data to determine which standards need attention, he is not efficiently using time to target specific areas of need. Finally, giving homework for which the students are not ready to practice independently frustrates the learners and the parents. Expecting parents to have the conceptual or procedural knowledge needed to teach or reinforce math concepts and problem-solving skills is unrealistic.

Secondary Example of Long-Term Practice Before Tests

The learning targets for this secondary example are: 1) *read and compre-hend complex literary and informational text independently and proficiently* (CCR Anchor Standard 10 for Reading) and 2) *write routinely in a single sit-ting for a range of tasks, purposes, and audiences* (CCR Anchor Standard 10 for Writing).

It is the beginning of the school year, and the tenth-grade team of teach-ers is meeting together to review the results of the state test that the students took late in the previous spring. The results are disappointing: a new set of standards is proving to be more challenging to master. The English teacher proposes that the ninth-grade team (English, social studies, science, and math) work together this year on something she calls *literacy rehearsal*. She explains that literacy rehearsal differs from activities such as sustained silent reading in which students read books of their own choosing. To qualify for literacy rehearsal, the books and articles students read must relate to content in the various disciplines, and students must be prepared to write in response to what they have read using a literacy process.

The English teacher goes on to explain that her version of literacy rehearsal is connected to two of the CCR Anchor Standards. Reading Anchor Standard 10 calls for sustained opportunities for reading to learn from expos-itory informational text such as content textbooks, literary informational text (literary nonfiction), and narrative texts (fiction). Literacy rehearsal requires concentration and effort. It involves reading and intensively thinking about a text to determine whether the author's reasoning about a claim is valid and the evidence is relevant and sufficient. It also entails the close, careful, and thoughtful reading of texts. The English teacher makes a convincing case for sustained practice in reading and writing across all departments and teams if students are to develop the fluency and endurance they need to meet the demands of the tests.

The team brainstorms various ways this kind of sustained practice could be organized across their four different disciplines, and they also identify some way to schedule the practice so that it is sustained, but not overly bur-densome, to either faculty or students. The teachers agree that all students will have to read books or articles that are specific to each discipline and that all texts will be nonfiction since that is a school-wide emphasis for the coming year. They agree that one day each week all of the students on their team will experience one period of reading and responding to what they have read in writing. During Week 1, the English teacher will teach a full day of literacy rehearsal with literary nonfiction. Week 2, the math teacher will teach a full day of literacy rehearsal in all his classes and have students read articles or book chapters about mathematics topics. Week 3 will be the science teacher's turn, and during Week 4, the social studies teacher will conduct the literacy rehearsal. The teachers develop a menu of ways that students can respond in writing to what they have read to include choosing one of several appropriate prompts and responding with a constructed response. At the end of the first month, students will take a short assessment that includes reading a passage and writing a brief response. The team has developed a rubric for them to use to evaluate the responses. During the second month, each of the teachers will team teach a larger group, and students will have small group focus lessons on various strategies. They agree to evaluate their schedule at the end of the second month and tweak any problems that have not already been solved.

Secondary Nonexample of Long-Term Practice Before Tests

The nonexample teacher is preparing her students for the summative test in which they will read essays and speeches and then be asked to identify the position and support for the author's viewpoint. Students have been given extensive notes on persuasive techniques and types of reasoning. However, they have had few opportunities to actually thoroughly read and process a variety of essays and speeches and then write in response to what they have read. The day prior to the test, the teacher hands out a test review sheet consisting of vocabulary terms, definitions, and two- or three-line excerpts from various historical documents. Students work with partners and use their notes to match terms with definitions and examples. For homework, the teacher gives students a passage to read and ten questions to answer that the teacher believes will be on the test. In this nonexample classroom, most of the practice time is devoted to retrieval and comprehension of declarative knowledge. The homework assignment provides some element of practicing procedural knowledge, but without close monitoring by the teacher or in varied texts. Lecturing, providing notes, and giving out a test review of the learning targets or content is not enough. Students must have many opportunities over time to construct understanding and use the procedural knowledge to develop as fluent, critical readers and writers.

Determining If Students Improve Their Test Performance Through Practice

The feedback you receive from your students' performances on the tests they take is one way you can determine if your practice sessions before the test were beneficial. Here is a list of ways you can monitor whether your students are ready for a summative test as a result of the practice sessions you have provided:

- Students can paraphrase or summarize the critical or essential elements of a skill, strategy, or process.

- Students can describe how, why, and when to use a specific skill, strategy, or process.

- Students can describe the relationship between the components or steps in a skill, strategy, or process.

- Students can execute the components of the skill, strategy, or process.

- Students are able to handle varied practice independently.

The student proficiency scale for practicing before a test in Figure 6.2 can help you assess how well your students are progressing toward the desired result. Use the scale to help you monitor for the desired result.

Table 6.2: Student Proficiency Scale for Practicing Before Tests

Emerging	Fundamental	Desired Result
Students are aware of the knowledge or skill they are practicing.	Students identify and commit to personal learning goals related to their mastery of standards and track their progress toward the learning goal during practice.	Students state how the practice session is aligned to their learning goal and how it can help them make progress toward it.
Students use procedural knowledge during practice.	Students use procedural knowledge in a variety of situations during practice.	Students fluently recall and apply procedural knowledge in a variety of situations during practice.
Students understand skills, strategies, and processes.	Students identify the skill, strategy, or process to use on test questions.	Students intentionally select and use the skill, strategy, or process for each test question.

Scaffold and Extend Instruction to Meet Students' Needs

Some students need additional support to prepare for testing, while others may be able to engage in self-evaluation, fine-tuning complex processes to perfection. You will need to develop materials that provide varied practice as well as additional help for students who need support. Here are some ideas for developing scaffolding and extending activities to meet students' needs.

Scaffolding

- Provide students with a video of the steps in various types of procedural knowledge that you can replay as needed to help break down information into digestible chunks.

- Have students create their own video or audio recording of the steps of a process.

Extending

- Students who are already well prepared for the test can benefit from refining and tuning their procedural knowledge by engaging in thought-provoking discussions and creating test-like questions.

- Have students work with the more rigorous standards on a complex text to design multiple-choice and open-ended response questions, along with the answer key and study guide for other students.

- Once questions are created, have the students align the questions with the learning targets to determine whether the questions match the level of thinking required to demonstrate mastery.

- Ensure that accelerated students are able to slow down and check their work and read more deliberately if needed to find evidence and support in the text.

Conclusion

The goal of this guide is to enable teachers to become more effective in designing and implementing practice techniques to help their students achieve content proficiencies. The beginning step, as you have learned in the preceding pages, is to become skilled at helping your students develop proficiency by practicing skills, strategies, and processes.

To determine whether this goal has been met, you will need to gather information from your students, as well as solicit feedback from your supervisor or colleagues, to find someone willing to embark on this learning journey with you. Engage in a meaningful self-reflection on your use of the strategy. If you acquire nothing else from this book, let it be the importance of *monitoring*. The tipping point in your level of expertise and your students' achievement is *monitoring*. Implementing this strategy well is not enough. Your goal is the desired result: evidence that your students have developed a deeper understanding of the content by practicing skills, strategies, and processes.

To be most effective, view implementation as a three-step process:

1. Implement the strategy using your energy and creativity to adopt and adapt the various techniques in this guide.

2. Monitor for the desired result. In other words, while you are implementing the technique, determine whether that technique is effective with the students. Check in real time to immediately see or hear whether your students are building fluency and gaining confidence and competence in their execution of skills, strategies, and processes.

3. If, as a result of your monitoring, you realize that your instruction was not adequate for students to achieve the desired result, seek out ways to change and adapt.

Although you can certainly experience this guide and gain expertise independently, the process will be more beneficial if you read and work through its contents with colleagues.

Reflection and Discussion Questions

Use the following reflection and discussion questions during a team meeting or even as food for thought prior to a meeting with your coach, mentor, or supervisor:

1. How has your instruction changed as a result of reading and implementing the instructional techniques found in this book?

2. What ways have you found to modify and enhance the instructional techniques found in this book to scaffold and extend your instruction?

3. What was your biggest challenge, in terms of implementing this instructional strategy?

4. How would you describe the changes in your students' learning that have occurred as a result of implementing this instructional strategy?

5. What will you do to share what you have learned with colleagues at your grade level or in your department?

References

Common Core State Standards Initiative. (2010). *Common Core state standards for English language arts & literacy in history/social studies, science, and technical subjects.* Washington, DC: Author. Retrieved November 24, 2014, from http://corestandards.org/assets/CCSI_ELA%20Standards.pdf

Crawford, D. (n.d.). *The third stage of learning math facts: Developing automaticity.* Eau Claire, WI: Otter Creek Institute. Retrieved February 11, 2015, from https://www.oci-sems.com/ContentHTML/pdfs/Research%20and%20Results.pdf

Dash, J. (2000). *The longitude prize.* New York: Farrar, Straus and Giroux.

Heiligman, D. (1996). *From caterpillar to butterfly.* New York: HarperCollins.

McEwan, E. K. (2009). *Teach them all to read: Catching kids before they fall through the cracks.* Thousand Oaks, CA: Corwin.

McEwan-Adkins, E. K. (2010). *40 reading intervention strategies for K–6 students: Research-based support for RTI.* Bloomington IN: Solution Tree Press.

McEwan-Adkins, E. K., & Burnett, A. J. (2012). *20 literacy strategies to meet the Common Core.* Bloomington, IN: Solution Tree Press.

Magana, S., & Marzano, R. J. (2013). *Enhancing the art and science of teaching with technology.* Bloomington, IN: Marzano Research Laboratory.

Marzano, R. J. (2007). *The art and science of teaching,* Alexandria, VA: ASCD.

Marzano, R. J. (2009). *Designing and teaching learning goals and objectives.* Bloomington, IN: Marzano Research Laboratory.

Marzano, R. J., T. Boogren, T., Heflebower, T., Kanold-McIntyre, J., & Pickering, D. (2012). *Becoming a reflective teacher.* Bloomington, IN: Marzano Research Laboratory.

Marzano, R. J., & Kendal, J. S. (2006). *The new taxonomy of educational objectives.* Thousand Oaks, CA: Corwin.

Marzano, R. J., & Pickering, D. (2001). *Classroom strategies that work.* Alexandria, VA: ASCD.

Marzano, R. J., & Toth, M. D. (2013). *Deliberate practice for deliberate growth: Teacher evaluation systems for continuous instructional improvement.* West Palm Beach, FL: Learning Sciences International.

Merlin, P. (2000). The coyote. In S. J. Phillips & P. W. Comus (Eds.), *A natural history of the Sonoran Desert* (p. 37). Tucson, AZ: Arizona-Sonoran Desert Museum Press and Berkeley, CA: University of California Press.

National Governors Association Center for Best Practices, Council of Chief State School Officers. (2010). *Common Core State Standards.* Washington, DC: Author.

NGSS Lead States. 2013. *Next Generation Science Standards: For states, by states.* Washington, DC: The National Academies Press.

Rasinski, T. V., Padak, N., Linke, W., & Sturdevant, E. (1994). The effects of fluency development instruction on urban second graders. *Journal of Education Research, 87,* 158–164.

Renkl, A. (1997). Learning from worked-out examples: A study on individual differences. *Cognitive Science, 21*(1), 1–29.

Stein, M., Silbert, J., & Carnine, D. (1997). *Designing effective mathematics instruction: A direct instruction approach,* 3rd ed. Upper Saddle River, NJ: Prentice Hall.

Index

Notes

Notes

MARZANO CENTER

Essentials for Achieving Rigor SERIES

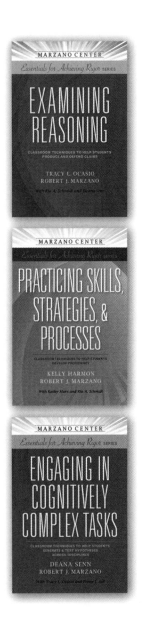

EXAMINING REASONING
Classroom Techniques to Help Students Produce and Defend Claims
TRACY L. OCASIO
ROBERT J. MARZANO
With Ria A. Schmidt and Deana Senn

PRACTICING SKILLS, STRATEGIES, & PROCESSES
Classroom Techniques to Help Students Develop Proficiency
KELLY HARMON
ROBERT J. MARZANO
With Kathy Marx and Ria A. Schmidt

ENGAGING IN COGNITIVELY COMPLEX TASKS
Classroom Techniques to Help Students Generate & Test Hypotheses Across Disciplines
DEANA SENN
ROBERT J. MARZANO
With Tracy L. Ocasio and Peter L. Sell

IDENTIFYING CRITICAL CONTENT
Classroom Techniques to Help Students Know What Is Important
DEANA SENN
AMBER C. RUTHERFORD
ROBERT J. MARZANO

EXAMINING SIMILARITIES & DIFFERENCES
Classroom Techniques to Help Students Deepen Their Understanding
CONNIE SCOLES WEST
ROBERT J. MARZANO
With Kathy Marx and Tracy L. Sell

PROCESSING NEW INFORMATION
Classroom Techniques to Help Students Engage With Content
TZEPORAW SAHADEO-TURNER
ROBERT J. MARZANO
With Gwendolyn L. Bryant and Kelly Harmon

Creating & Using LEARNING TARGETS & PERFORMANCE SCALES
How Teachers Make Better Instructional Decisions
CARLA MOORE
LIBBY H. GARST
ROBERT J. MARZANO
With Elizabeth Kennedy and Deana Senn

RECORDING & REPRESENTING KNOWLEDGE
Classroom Techniques to Help Students Examine Their Deeper Understanding
RIA A. SCHMIDT
ROBERT J. MARZANO
With Libby H. Garst and Laurine Halter

REVISING KNOWLEDGE
Classroom Techniques to Help Students Examine Their Deeper Understanding
RIA A. SCHMIDT
ROBERT J. MARZANO
With Laurine Halter, Tracy L. Ocasio, and Deana Senn

ORGANIZING FOR LEARNING
Classroom Techniques to Help Students Interact Within Small Groups
DEANA SENN
ROBERT J. MARZANO
With Libby H. Garst and Carla Moore

LearningSciencesInternational
LEARNING AND PERFORMANCE MANAGEMENT

Visit www.education-store.learningsciences.com or call 877-411-7114